# COMEDY
# WRITING

**Jenny Roche**

**TEACH YOURSELF BOOKS**

For UK orders: please contact Bookpoint Ltd, 39 Milton Park, Abingdon, Oxon OX14 4TD. Telephone: (44) 01235 400414, Fax: (44) 01235 400454. Lines are open from 9.00–6.00, Monday to Saturday, with a 24 hour message answering service. Email address: orders@bookpoint.co.uk

For USA & Canada orders: please contact NTC/Contemporary Publishing, 4255 West Touhy Avenue, Lincolnwood, Illinois 60646–1975, USA. Telephone: (847) 679 5500, Fax: (847) 679 2494.

Long renowned as the authoritative source for self-guided learning – with more than 30 million copies sold worldwide – the *Teach Yourself* series includes over 200 titles in the fields of languages, crafts, hobbies, business and education.

*British Library Cataloguing in Publication Data*
A catalogue entry for this title is available from The British Library.

*Library of Congress Catalog Card Number:* On file

First published in UK 1999 by Hodder Headline Plc, 338 Euston Road, London, NW1 3BH.

First published in US 1999 by NTC/Contemporary Publishing, 4255 West Touhy Avenue, Lincolnwood (Chicago), Illinois 60646–1975 USA.

The 'Teach Yourself' name and logo are registered trade marks of Hodder & Stoughton Ltd.

Copyright © 1999 Jenny Roche

Cover photo: Barbara Baran

Typeset by Transet Limited, Coventry, England.
Printed in Great Britain for Hodder & Stoughton Educational, a division of Hodder Headline Plc, 338 Euston Road, London NW1 3BH by Cox & Wyman Ltd, Reading, Berkshire.

Impression number    10 9 8 7 6 5 4 3 2 1
Year                            2004 2003 2002 2001 2000 1999

# CONTENTS

# ACKNOWLEDGEMENTS

Copyright Permission and Rights Acknowledgements to: Richard Bell, *Writers News*, for permission to quote from my articles; Carol Barton for the 'Gran' cartoon strip.

Thanks to BBC Bristol's Animation Unit, for information on animation.

Special thanks must go to Alan McDonald, my first creative writing tutor, whose encouragement made me think I could write, who set the assignment for a piece of work which became my first fiction sale, and who determined the direction of my future writing life by asking, 'Have you ever thought of writing straight comedy?'

For keeping me going in that direction, thanks go to Dave McKeon whose ideas, thoughts and discussion helped clarify my notions of comedy. Thanks also for his help in reading through the drafts of this book.

Thanks to Comedy Writers Association UK and all its members for contacts, resources and the compulsion to be professional.

Thanks to Keith Birch at Liverpool University Department of Continuing Education for the opportunity to do the teaching from which I learnt so much, and to all the students on my courses and workshops who assisted in my education.

Finally, this book is dedicated to my daughter Laura and son Colm, who have contributed more than positively to my philosophy on life.

# 1 | INTRODUCTION

*If you have a sense of humour, if things appear funny to you, if you think you can write, you can.*

**Gene Perret**

You may be reading this book because you feel you have a talent for writing comedy or you may want to improve or develop the skills you already have. You may be a stand-up comedian wanting to write your own material, or a writer wanting to enhance another form of writing through the use of humour. Whatever your interest in comedy writing, the aim of this book is to make the subject relevant to all levels of ability and experience.

## Can comedy be taught?

There are some who say the ability to make people laugh is a natural gift which you have either got or you haven't. To say this, however, is like saying there is nothing to learn, and it would be difficult to find the successful comedy writer who can say it was all down to natural ability, and on the road to success he or she never learnt anything about the art and craft of his or her discipline.

The skills of a comedy writer – the creation, shaping and honing of comedy material, knowledge of market requirements, the understanding of why some jokes make people laugh and others do not – are far from being skills which are an innate attribute or some will-o'-the-wisp phenomenon: they are a craft with elements which can be learnt. This places comedy writing within the grasp of anyone who has a sense of humour they wish to develop, and a willingness to have a go.

This is not to say the art and craft of being able to make someone smile or laugh out loud is a particularly easy one: what is funny and what is not, is a highly subjective area. The aim of this book, however, is to demystify both the nature of comedy and the processes which go into its creation.

Intended as a practical guide to writing rather than a theoretical or definitive authority on the subject of comedy, the book aims not to stifle creativity by saying this is how comedy should or should not be written, but rather to show you the basic tools of comedy writing and how to use them. You can, and should, use and develop your own unique style.

With the emphasis being on the practical, this book will help you to develop and sharpen your comedy writing skills and as you progress through the pages you should become more confident, capable and professional in your approach.

# The scope for comedy material

Comedy is a major commodity today and not only are there market outlets clearly defined as comedy – jokes, sketches, sitcoms, etc – a comedy writer's skills are increasingly being called upon in the worlds of advertising, promotion, publicity, business, training, education and other areas as a means of getting information, advice and messages across in a more interesting, entertaining and easily absorbed way.

Magazine editors, publishers and TV and radio producers also have a constant request for more humour in fiction, non-fiction and drama, with the result that the writer who can add a touch of humour to his or her work is a writer with a better than average chance of success.

Comedy writers are very much in demand and once the basic principles of writing comedy and understanding market requirements are achieved, there are many market outlets for their work.

# How to use this book

The book begins with the writing of shorter forms of comedy and progresses to longer forms, before diversifying into writing for the different areas of comedy and humour. Along the way there is guidance on writing for various mediums such as radio, TV and theatre.

It is not within the scope of this book, however, to go into great detail about the specific technical requirements of each medium, as there are many books available which deal with this in depth. Several companion volumes in the *Teach Yourself* series will be useful in this respect and other titles, but by no means a comprehensive list, are mentioned in the appendices. The emphasis in this book is on providing the basic knowledge and understanding for you to be able to write in these areas, while giving more detailed guidance on how and where comedy can be used to best advantage.

Chapters 2–4 cover the understanding of comedy and the basics of beginning writing and should be read first, as they are relevant to all forms of comedy writing. Other chapters may be read out of sequence if you are interested in a particular aspect of comedy writing.

You may find it useful, however, to read the chapters on one-liners and sketch writing before doing this as they will help with shaping and structuring comedy ideas. Both forms offer good experience in using different comedy techniques.

Some chapters are intended to be read in conjunction with another, for example, the chapters on writing for TV and radio are relevant to sketch and sitcom writing, and the information on dialogue in the writing for radio chapter is relevant to other comedy forms. To avoid repeating information, cross references indicate where you can find further information or explanation.

## The exercises

As no one can be called a comedy writer unless they actually write, in relevant sections there are opportunities to consolidate learning and put comedy writing into practice by the means of exercises.

## ⇒ To market

An important part of the comedy writer's life is knowing how and where to sell any work and there is no doubt that establishing good habits of first researching the market will save wasted time, energy and rejection slips. Each relevant section gives guidance on markets and marketing, indicated by the heading above.

As markets do constantly change, emerge and disappear I have tended not to be too specific. Instead, I have mentioned the range of outlets available, and offered suggestions as to how and where you can find more detailed and up-to-date information. I have also given advice on how to present your work, and there are further hints and tips to give you better chances of success. Where relevant I have shown how the same material can be adapted to fit alternative market outlets.

# Terms used

There is not always a consensus on the usage and meaning of some terms and words used in the comedy world, and where there may be a different term or word used this is indicated by the use of bracketed 'also-known-as ...' (aka) alternatives. The intention is not to be patronizing to those with more knowledge of the comedy world, but to help the newcomer.

For convenience, some blanket terms have been used:

**Comedian** to refer to both male and female comedy performers.

**A funny** (or **funnies**) to refer collectively to gags, jokes, wisecracks, funny observations, comments and anecdotes, silences, and physical comedy including looks, stares, stumbles, shrugs of the shoulders, a custard pie in the face, etc. In fact anything, no matter how packaged, which is designed to make people laugh.

# 2 | THE NATURE OF COMEDY

Giving consideration to how and why comedy makes people laugh, or not laugh, is not merely an academic exercise. Understanding the nature of comedy and laughter will enable you to gain valuable insights, which will give greater control over your comedy writing.

A comedy writer has to be a master juggler, keeping many balls in the air, for comedy to be both relevant and accessible to an audience. The difficulty when looking at the nature of comedy, however, is that it is hardly a precise science.

Research attempting to analyse and quantify the peculiarly human phenomena of comedy, and the laughter it produces, has been undertaken by many academics including psychologists, philosophists, linguists, anthropologists, educationists, sociologists, mathematicians and countless others. They have put forward many theories, but no general principles have been found to be applicable to all occasions. Comedy is such a subjective, multi-faceted area that while the studies are of great interest, there is a need to give them the context of a practical basis. From the point of view of a comedian or a comedy writer, the studies are best summed up by these comments on one researcher:

> The trouble with Freud is that he never had to play the old Glasgow
> Empire on a Saturday night after Rangers and Celtic had both lost.
>
> Ken Dodd

Trying to analyse comedy has been described as trying to catch smoke. Difficult, yes, but we do all know what smoke looks like and can find ways to channel it up a chimney or put it into a container. We will go on to the channelling and containing of comedy in subsequent sections, but let's first look at the substance of that smoke.

# The need for laughter

> We need commentators. They talk about the madness of the world ...
> as we get crazier, more and more comedians will come along and tell
> us we're crazy.
>
> Steve Allen in *How to be Funny*

> ... it is equally true to say that modern life has brought in its train
> increased anxiety and strain ... the public longs for a quiet respite
> amid the cares and exasperating pressure of the workaday world.
> Thus the gift of laughter ... is today doubly precious.
>
> AA Thomson in *Written Humour*

Comedy is entertainment, and laughter has been seen as escapism from a
world which can often be bad and mad. It is interesting to note that the
first quote was written in 1992, while the second was written in 1936.
Perhaps nothing much changes and comedy and laughter will always
satisfy a basic human need to escape from the everyday world. The good
news is, if trends continue, there will always be a need for comedy writers
and comedians.

> Comedy can unwind people's hang-ups. It can also reassure and
> comfort, massage egos and, at its simplest, cheer people up.
>
> Barry Took

Comedy helps us to relax and unwind not only by allowing us to escape.
By approaching from an oblique angle, it encourages us to see the
incongruities and oddities of life, and offers an alternative view of the
world.

> Do not adjust your perspective, there is a fault in reality.
>
> Anon

Not so much escapism as facing things head on, satire, that most potent
form of political and social comedy, challenges and exposes the
hypocrisies, lies and shams in the political and social worlds. Less
aggressive in nature, a stand-up comedian's observational material
questions the whys and wherefores of the ordinary and everyday.

> Have you ever noticed when you're with someone and they taste
> something really bad, they always want you to taste it immediately.
> 'That's horrible, here, taste it.'
>
> Ellen DeGeneres

Comedy is much more than escapism, however. Recommended by doctors and therapists and used in laughter clinics, comedy has benefits for both our physical and mental welfare.

# The therapeutic nature of comedy

It is true that the person with a sense of humour tends to be more relaxed and therefore better able to avoid stress-related health problems, but this does not even cover half the benefits of laughter ...

> Laughter seems to be able to reduce muscle tension, relax the sympathetic nervous system, bring down high blood pressure ... helps to increase circulation and energy through the body ... releases endorphins, which is the body's natural painkiller ... it has been found that laughter actually boosts the immune system.
>
> Robert Holden, psychotherapist

If laughter is medicine then a comedy writer, in providing the stimulus for that laughter, has to get the formula right and deliver it in the right dosage, cajoling the 'patient' if necessary.

# The laughter triangle

It shouldn't be thought, however, that getting the right formula and dosage will automatically lead to laughter. There are many variables determining whether a funny will make someone laugh, so there is no straightforward equation of comedy = laughter. It is much better to think in terms of a triangular model.

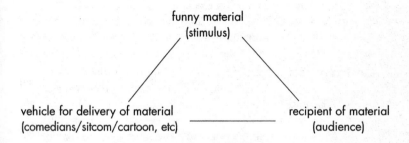

**Figure 2.1    The laughter triangle**

All three points of the triangle need to be on target and connected to each other before there can be the potential for laughter.

- ■ The funny material has to be not only well written, but appropriately targeted towards the vehicle and the recipient.
- ■ The recipient has to be understood and the mood gauged and carefully manipulated with the right material, delivered in the right way.
- ■ The vehicle will determine how and in what form the material should be delivered, keeping in mind who the recipient is to be.

The application of this triangular model will become relevant in later sections when we look at relating material to the mediums in which it is to be delivered, and how a stand-up comic relates to an audience.

We will look now at some of the situations in which comedy is created in everyday life and consider how this can be translated into comedy as entertainment.

# Comedy as a coping mechanism

I force myself to laugh at everything, for fear of being compelled to weep.

Pierre August de Beaumarchais, French dramatist

The idea that if you don't laugh, you'll cry, is sometimes given as an explanation for the humour of the powerless, the oppressed and the disadvantaged. Somewhat patronizing, given the rich veins of humour which have been mined by comedians who are Jewish, black, Asian, gay, unemployed, female or disabled, for example. The same idea can, however, be used to explain why we might find ourselves laughing when the occasion is anything but funny; for instance funeral wakes are often beset with laughter.

Comedy can be used to release the tension in uncomfortable or difficult situations. If it is a dark, scary night, for example, and we are worried and anxious, if a friend then shouts boo! we may find ourselves laughing, not because the situation is funny, but because there is an a opportunity to release the tension we have been feeling. The more nervous, anxious or embarrassed we are, the more likely we are to laugh or giggle at the least little thing.

However, this response would not be considered appropriate in such tense, nervous situations as a driving test, or when meeting someone for the first time. Any laughter here has to be more controlled. The friendly gesture of a smile, or a touch of humorous banter, can release tension by breaking the ice and reducing social distance, so bringing about a more relaxed atmosphere.

Tuning into the appropriateness of real life humour will help you to develop an instinct for the applications of truth and humanity in your comedy writing.

In life, if there is an awkward or embarrassing moment, a humorous comment is a flipping over of the comedy coin to see the situation in a different way. Flipping the coin isn't the same as being flippant, however – it is not just about dismissing the situation, 'laughing it off' or cracking a joke with no connection to the situation. This could be seen as subverting or diverting attention away from the situation. There may be two sides to the coin but they are still part of the same coin.

For the situation to be defused effectively, the humorous response has to be relevant, appropriate and truthful to life, its situations and its characters. Having the same aims for any funnies you write will always render them more effective in the laughter stakes.

# Comic distancing

> Most humour is based on fear. When you laugh at a man upended by
> a banana skin, you laugh because you're so jolly glad it wasn't you.
>
> Ronnie Barker

We can all relate to the misfortunes and predicaments of others but are less likely to laugh if the person suffers real harm or injury. The same principle applies to comedy entertainment and in cartoons where characters may be flattened, blown to pieces or otherwise injured. We laugh because no real harm is suffered and the character is returned to normal in a short while.

Making situations or characters surreal or extraordinary can also create a comic distancing. The situation of Vyvyan in the TV sitcom 'The Young Ones' being decapitated after sticking his head out of a train window, in ordinary circumstances, would be horrific. However, in the extraordinary world of 'The Young Ones', Vyvyan gets off the train to retrieve his head, and, when it is abusive, kicks it along the track. Here there is also another kind of distancing, not from the situation of somebody literally losing their head, but from the exaggerated characterization of the kind of person who would do that.

## Taboo topics

Topics such as death, disease and disability are sensitive and we need to decide how to handle them without being nauseous or offensive. There is no subject which cannot be considered as potential comedy material, but it does depend on the angle of approach.

You may have to work harder to find humour in taboo topics but the use of lateral thinking will enable you to find other, less sensitive angles that will provide targets for your comedy. For example, a war is not funny in itself, but perhaps the silly comings and goings and ludicrous decisions of politicians and the military may be fruitful areas for a comic interpretation. (See also Chapter 3, Beginning comedy writing – Generating ideas.)

The only prerequisite when targeting sensitive or controversial subjects in comedy is that there should be truth in what you are saying and, of course, it should be funny. The mad, bad things in the world can become the source of comedy material but if we think of them as being on one side of that comedy coin mentioned earlier, then we need to be able to see the funny side on the reverse.

## Insult humour

When we joke about our bosses or figures of authority, the joke may be based on the things we cannot say to their faces, or the things we wish we had said, but could only think of later. It may be that we think those people deserve to be put down through insult, along with pompous and pretentious and disruptive people, such as hecklers.

There is, however, a narrow dividing line between hurt and humour and if an insult is too scathing, too venomous or attacking, it will not work as it will have overstepped the mark by becoming aggressive. In the case of hecklers it could make the situation worse.

In addition to being truthful, insult humour should always be funny and non-antagonistic. Go for mild jostling rather than the jugular. (See also Chapter 13, Stand-up comedy – Hecklebusters.)

# Stereotypes

There was an Englishman, an Irishman and a Scotsman ...
The set-up for many a joke using stereotypes

Comedy has a long history of scapegoating certain groups, and each country has its own stock scapegoat. When used by a dominant group, funnies based on stereotypes can be unpleasant and offensive. Stereotypes are not in favour today; indeed many comedy clubs have a policy of no racist or sexist material.

It is very easy, however, to use stereotypes as a short-cut recognition symbol, which saves time in setting up a funny. Nevertheless, it is important to remember all stereotypes are negative and lack truth. It should also be considered how comedy can create and proliferate the ideas behind stereotypes, with the stereotypes then being used to justify discrimination and prejudice.

# Social control mechanism

When groups or individuals are picked upon for perhaps being no more than 'different', social norms can be shaped and a spurious status quo enforced.

There is a view that the use of stereotypes is a way of overcoming insecurity, a kind of one-upmanship and defensive mechanism. If we are ugly we can gain some kind of superiority by finding, or creating, someone who is uglier.

Ridiculing those who are intellectually, economically or socially superior, such as academics, entrepreneurs, the upper classes and royalty, to make them look silly and pretentious, can weaken their position and power in our eyes.

Trainspotters and stamp collectors may similarly be ridiculed, while the gregarious partygoer is glorified; 'softies' who watch daytime TV or soaps may be scorned in favour of the hardened beer-swigging sports addict.

If a particular individual, such as a personality or politician, or a group, for example, racial groups, women, or those with disabilities, has a distinguishing feature or habit then this will be seized upon, exaggerated and joked about to the point of the ridiculous. In all, you are being told this is how you should, or shouldn't look, or behave.

There is also the problem that cartoon caricaturists, comedy impressionists and satirists need to make use of distinguishing features for parody or mimicry. When writing for these outlets, thought should be given to how this can be done without perpetuating negative images. Due consideration should also be given to the laws of libel, defamation and slander.

## Safety valve

> Laughter helps control our negative emotions
>
> Steve Allen

There is a view that comedy is a safety valve for expressing grievances and controlling aggression. If the occasion, etiquette or the possibility of a punch in the mouth prevents us from saying what we would really like to say, then humour can often soften the approach, release the tension and make the respondent more amenable to what we have to say.

A stand-up comedian may be able to use the stage to complain or rant about the world but if we think of the triangle formula mentioned earlier, then those complaints and anger are not going to hit the mark and produce laughter unless the audience can relate to feeling angry and annoyed about the same kinds of things.

> There's a point when you can get too angry on stage and then the audience is frightened by your anger, you have to walk a tightrope.
>
> Joy Behar

## Banana skins

In a sketch or film we might laugh at someone stepping on a banana skin, slipping and ending up on their bottom. If it is a pompous or arrogant person we laugh because it is right they should be brought down. If it is a nun in a starched habit who slips, we laugh because the fall is incongruous to the strict regime of a religious order.

If an overweight person slips we might have laughed at one time – being fat was considered sociably undesirable. However, now that more people are worried about their weight, eating disorders are recognized and we have a more enlightened attitude, an overweight person falling is not considered quite so funny.

If a frail elderly lady slips we might not be so quick to laugh, as she does not deserve to fall. If she hurts herself we are even less likely to laugh. There needs to be distancing to make the situation funny, perhaps by manipulation of the character and/or the situation, for example, if the elderly woman is a cartoon character, a crook in disguise or Supergran momentarily delayed by an adversary.

If we look on comedy as being that banana skin, and the person stepping onto it as the target of a joke, then we should think carefully about the targets of our funnies if we want to be both responsible in our humour, and get the most laughs.

# Comedy as a non-aggressive tool

> I know that having the ability to make fun of my negative personality traits has defused many a fight with my loved ones.
>
> Judy Carter

Humour is a powerful social tool which many people can use to advantage. For example, real estate agents and salespeople use it to relax customers and make them feel less threatened; auditioning actors and job interviewees to make themselves remembered in a positive and friendly way.

Being able to flip the comedy coin to find this kind of humour can create a different atmosphere or set another agenda, which then gives the coin flipper greater control over a given situation, even when it is threatening. There are people who, when confronted with anger, aggression or violence, through presence of mind and the courage to keep calm, have been able to disarm their aggressors with a humorous quip. Take, for instance, the woman speaking on a TV documentary who described how she and a friend when confronted by two men, one of whom exposed himself, said, 'What a pity I haven't got a pair of scissors, we could have had sausage for tea.' The man, surprised by the unexpected reaction, didn't know how to respond, and was effectively disarmed long enough for the women to leave.

This is not to say that anybody in a threatening or dangerous situation should always resort to humour. If the woman had made the comment in an aggressive or challenging tone, or if some things had been different, there might not have been such a favourable ending. On this occasion the woman had seen a humorous connection, and was able to set another agenda to that of threats and fear. She had read both the situation and the man, was able to flip the comedy coin, and see a different perspective.

When writing comedy it is a similar reading of, or rather setting up of, situation and character which makes for appropriate and truthful humour. If we see the woman's response as a punchline we can perceive how it has the vital component of any punchline – surprise.

# No butts

Sometimes we laugh when there is no obvious joke or funny situation. We laugh when we are tickled, when we engage in social banter and when we are just enjoying ourselves at parties and other occasions. It is just pure fun and happiness and there is a parallel within the comedy world with funnies which do not have a target or a butt of the joke.

Funnies based on word play, slapstick, clowning, custard pies in the face and other forms of knockabout and harmless physical humour, all give the opportunity to fool around like children again. It is simple silliness and a certain chance to escape that mad, bad world. Circus clowns are the epitome of comedy without a target, while sitcoms such as 'The Young Ones' and 'Bottom' often took slapstick to its extreme.

# Social context

Comedy is social interaction between the giver and the receiver; it is subject matter evolving from life and being given back to life, albeit in a different form.

Poetry or prose can be written for your own pleasure but comedy is the only form of writing where you cannot be a secret scribbler. Comedy demands social interaction by the response of laughter from another person.

If we look at this interactive process and its social settings we can see how the laughter response is more easily gained in certain circumstances. This will be useful in predisposing an audience to laughter, and in considering how to make comedy material hit the funny bone in an audience.

## Laughter is infectious

> Laugh and the whole world laughs with you.
>
> Ella Wheeler Wilcox,
> American journalist and writer

As anyone who has ever found themselves laughing when confronted with a puppet clown laughing endlessly at a theme park will testify, laughter is infectious.

This can be useful when a comedian's laughter at his or her own jokes sets off a similar response in an audience. It is also useful to have someone who laughs loudly in the audience of a TV comedy recording, who can set everybody else off. There is discussion as to whether a studio audience is good or bad, but the thinking behind the lift that can be given to a comedy by a studio audience's laughter infecting a TV viewer at home, can be appreciated.

As mentioned previously, there are certain shared perceptions of when it is right to laugh, and when it is not right. This group concept means that sometimes we also need confirmation that it is all right to laugh. Saying 'here is a comedian', 'I'm going to tell you a joke now', or denoting a venue is a comedy club, are clearly defined ways of indicating approval of laughter, and if we do not laugh, it is not taken too lightly. There are, of course, many things which will affect whether an audience laughs or not and these will be discussed later. (See also Chapter 13, Stand-up Comedy – Material and the audience.)

In situations less clearly defined as comedic, we may sometimes wait to see if others laugh first. If they do, we will follow their example and if we do not think the item funny, we may laugh or smile out of politeness, or because we do not want to be thought unsociable or lacking in a sense of humour. The more intimate the exchange – one-to-one as opposed to a large audience – the greater the pressure to respond in this way.

## Comedy needs surprises

When somebody wanting to tell a joke begins by asking, 'Have you heard the one about …' they know that the more a joke is heard the less funny it will be. Funnies rely on punchlines, surprises and the unexpected, so, of course, if the joke has been heard before, there is no surprise.

This has relevance for the recycling of old jokes and for the comedian who can take the same act to different audiences around the country, but who needs a constant source of new material once the act is exposed to a television audience numbering millions. The sitcom or comedy drama which relies on jokes will also suffer from decreasing funniness, whereas those relying on character and situation will survive repeating viewing.

# Subjectivity of humour

It is said that everybody has a different sense of humour. It is impractical, however, for a comedy writer to write for every idiosyncrasy of humour in a large audience, but there are ways of making comedy relevant, understandable and appropriate to the greatest number of people.

## Cultural reference points

It is useful to be aware of particular words, objects, people and topics which have particular humorous relevance, associations, or just sound funny.

> … Alka Seltzer is funny. You say 'Alka Seltzer' you get a laugh …
> words with 'K' in them are funny. Casey Stengel, that's a funny
> name. Robert Taylor is not funny. Cupcake is funny. Tomato is
> funny. Cookie is funny. Cucumber is funny …
>
> Willy in *The Sunshine Boys* by Neil Simon

Objects which are funny and offer comic potential do so because of their particular associations – zimmer frames with getting old, take-aways with laziness and slobbiness, designer labels with the pretentious, green wellingtons and waxed jackets with upper crust country dwellers and Mills and Boon books with slushy romances. These objects are much easier to make fun of and use in connection with comedy than, say, apple pie, coal fires and roses which have associations with warm, homely, and loving things.

The people and topics of contemporary and topical interest and concern will have the most relevance to an audience, so it is useful to keep up with current issues and trends to know what is 'in' and what is 'out' of public interest and favour.

The particular words, objects, people and topics with humorous associations will change over time and vary with different cultures, and even different age groups within the same culture. Reading newspapers and magazines, watching television, talking and listening to people, will enable you to keep in touch with all that is culturally relevant and will enable you to make your comedy writing more accessible to an audience.

To do this entails knowing as much about your audience as you can, avoiding the excesses of offensive and insensitive material and, of course, writing good, strong, funny material.

---

**EXERCISES**

1 Compile lists of ten flowers, foods and household objects which are funny sounding or have funny associations. (Some crossword dictionaries and thesauruses have categorized lists which may be useful.)

2 Compile lists of five personalities from each of the worlds of music, entertainment, film/TV, sport and current affairs/politics. In a few words, summarize the aspects of their personality or situation they are best known for. For example, Charlie Chaplin – sad, poignant humour; Margaret Thatcher – the Iron Lady, tough dragon.

Keep hold of these lists and update them regularly. You will be able to use them when writing sketches, one-liners and stand-up material.

# 3 | BEGINNING COMEDY WRITING

## What is a comedy writer – the facts and the fallacies

There is a common fallacy that to be a comedy writer you need to be a funny person. You do need to be good with words and visual imagery, and an ability to know what sounds or looks funny is useful, but there is not the need for the extrovert personality of a comedian.

> I like to think you have to be miserable to be funny and vice versa. I suppose there are people who aren't miserable and are funny; an awful lot of the people I work with are miserable just by their very nature.
>
> Leslie Neilson

A comedian works in the public arena using natural or acquired performance skills. A comedy writer, on the other hand, works mostly in isolation using natural or acquired literary skills

### A comedy writer analyses and researches

> Humour is like a frog; if you dissect it, it dies.
>
> Mark Twain

With all due respect to Mark Twain, comedy is a highly competitive business and the writer, and indeed the comedy performer, who can adapt, change, and develop along with new trends and understands the nature of comedy and its constructions, is likely to have a longer and more successful career.

Whatever form of comedy writing you are dealing with – jokes, sketches, sitcoms, humorous articles or stories – analysis and dissection will give the knowledge and greater abilities to write in different styles. It will also allow you to identify and tap into different senses of humour and to work effectively with the words, images and relationships which can create something that, hopefully, will make people laugh.

Make analysing comedy a lifelong quest and look for how a funny is gained and the techniques used, not only in comedy shows and entertainment but in real life too. Every time you hear someone laugh, think about what has been said or done and in what circumstances.

Always be as objective as possible in any study of comedy; if there is something you don't find funny but others do, try to understand the reasons for their laughter. As a comedy writer you will need to be able to reach many different senses of humour, even if you have different tastes.

## Observation

It is important for a comedy writer to be a keen observer of life, as it is life's incongruities, oddities and peculiarities which provide the substance for comedy material. That material is static, however, if it is not brought alive by character.

A comedy writer should be a great 'people watcher' with a mental store, or notebook, filled with things people have said and done, the foibles, idiosyncrasies of individuals, the little tricks people use to cover their weaknesses and the battles won and lost in human conversation and interaction.

If you are just beginning to write comedy, the first exercise you should undertake is quite gentle: go about your everyday life, but with a greater awareness of what is going on around you – both the drama and the comedy. Also, read newspapers and magazines looking especially for human interest stories and those fascinating and odd little items which fill the small spaces left over from news or features articles.

## Responsibility

There is a very thin dividing line between comedy and tragedy, humour and hurt and a comedy writer should be understanding and astute enough to know when a situation or character is comedic and when it is not, when a joke is considered to be in good taste and when it isn't.

### Contentious material

Television regulatory bodies, broadcast monitoring organizations, print editors, comedy club and theatre managers, statutory laws, 'political correctness' and a comedy writer's own conscience all impose limits on the excesses of comedy material which is sexual in nature, contains bad language, is sexist, racist or deals with sensitive or controversial topics.

Any comedy writer or comedian who does have this kind of material is obviously treading on dangerous ground but it does not mean that it should be disregarded entirely. There is a very big market for risqué material in particular, and sometimes a bit of aggressive bad language can give an edge to a comedy act.

An audience is there to be entertained, however, and should not be alienated, offended or made to feel uncomfortable. It is a little different if they come along knowing there will be risqué jokes and bad language. For example, comedian Roy 'Chubby' Brown always plays to packed houses with material that can never be repeated on television, but his audience knows what to expect before they arrive.

The main requirement is that a comedy writer should not break any laws and should respect the decisions of venue managers, comedians and broadcasters to limit or refuse any contentious material.

## Professionalism

Having a professional attitude towards your work can make the difference between the comedy writer who is not only good, but is also successful.

You should have respect for both your writing and the people you are submitting to. Having a slapdash or negative attitude towards your work will not produce the best you are capable of and, while there is no doubt a lot of bad comedy does get through, cynicism towards the industry and the people in it should be avoided at all costs.

# Standard presentation

With all markets receiving far more submissions than can be bought, it is useful to put yourself in the position of the person who is going to receive and read your work and will be asking, 'Do I have the time, patience or inclination to read this when I have thousands of other submissions to read too?' Anything which can make your work easier to read will, of course, stand the better chance.

Each medium has its own specific requirements regarding how work should be laid out on the page, and details are given in the relevant sections of this book. However, there are certain criteria which should be met for all submissions, unless advised otherwise.

## Submitting material – standard presentation

It is the quality of the script or manuscript which gains a sale, not the cover. Script editors and readers are not impressed by gaudy covers or bindings, fancy typescripts, coloured paper or illustrations, clip art or other devices intended to make the script look pretty. They can see through any attempts to make a script stand out from others in the pile, and will probably read that script in a very negative light.

Standard presentation requires that:

- work should be typed/printed with a clean, clear typeface which is not blotchy or faint.
- white, standard size paper should be used. This should not be grubby, encrusted with coffee stains or show signs of having gone the rounds of many submissions to other places.
- margins should be wide – at least one inch each side, top and bottom.
- there should be no spelling or typing mistakes (aka typos). Use the spellcheck on your computer, or a dictionary. You may be able to get away with the occasional mistake, but they may interrupt the flow and rhythm. Also, as scripts are usually read quickly, anything which jars the reader or distracts his or her attention will make the job harder.
- your name and contact details should be included on all submissions – on a cover page for longer works, on every page for sketches and one-liners.
- all pages should be numbered.
- the correct layout should be used as this makes reading easier. The wrong layout makes it seem as though a piece of work has been submitted to the wrong medium.

## Stamped addressed envelopes

If you want your script to be returned it is usual to send a stamped, self-addressed envelope (aka SAE or SASE). Tight production schedules may lead to a policy of not returning material on topical shows and, a writer's brief should mention this.

If submitting to a foreign market, send a self-addressed envelope plus an International Reply Coupon for the postage. This will cover the cost of a basic rate airmail charge. If a script weighs more than this you will need to send the appropriate number of coupons. Your local librarian may be able to locate a reference book detailing foreign postage rates.

Alternatively, if you don't want the script to be returned, but would like to know its fate, send an envelope and an International Reply Coupon and request that you be informed of the decision, and the script destroyed if not accepted.

# Arrogance + humility = comedy writer

These may seem like two contradictory qualities but both are needed. A comedy writer needs to be arrogant in thinking he or she has the power to make people laugh with words, and also the humility to accept that he or she may not. Given the subjective nature of comedy, a writer will need a double dose of humility to accept that not everything he or she has written will be accepted. There will be rejection slips, even accomplished comedy writers get them, but there will also be acceptances.

# Generating ideas

Before you can have acceptances, you will need to have written something, and to write something you need ideas. A comedy writer cannot wait for ideas for good funnies to come along of their own accord: he or she needs to be a great 'ideas person' who can whistle up funnies whenever they are needed. This is especially important for the writer of shorter forms of comedy such as jokes and sketches, who will need to come up with lots of ideas, often at short notice.

## Inspirational aids

- *Notebook*   Keep a note of the odd thoughts, amusing incidents or observations you come across, or ideas which may just pop into your head.
- *Cuttings file*   Odd snippets and interesting stories from newspapers and magazines can provide inspiration for ideas and be worked into comedy material.

■ *Other comedy*   Watching, listening or reading comedy can give you ideas for other comedy, or you can 'switch' jokes and sketches.

(See also Chapter 5, One-liners – Switching.)

## Lateral thinking

Lateral thinking enables you to come up with ideas that are different, and by being so, they stand out from all the other submissions which land on a script reader's desk.

Constantly flip that comedy coin and search for new and original topics and fresh angles on old topics. Do not always be content with the first thing that comes into your head: continue searching until you have the strongest and most original premise you can think of.

## From connections to premise

In finding ideas for comedy material you will be looking for the connection, the things which go together to make the joke. The idea behind the connection will become the joke's premise, i.e. what it is about. You will see how to establish connections as we look at some techniques to generate ideas.

## Idea generating techniques

You beat your pate, and fancy wit will come. Knock as you please, there's nobody at home.

Alexander Pope

There are many different ways of generating ideas, some of which are outlined below. Find the one which works best for you, or fits the kind of comedy you are writing.

You need first to find a starting point for generating ideas. If you are working from a writer's brief for a comedy show, this will help focus on the sets, locations, characters, topics and so on to which you have to add comic incidents. If you have no writer's brief then you will first need to decide the focus for yourself. Topical material will take its starting point from a recent item of news.

You can find starting points by picking a word from a dictionary, turning to a page in the trade telephone directory, taking a phrase, cliché, song or book title, or preparing lists of subjects, objects and topics. The list you made for the exercises at the end of Chapter 2 can also be used.

Most idea generating techniques are based on brainstorming and free association of ideas until you find a connection. Think of anything and everything connected with your topic or subject. List the places, people, things, events, words, clichés, phrases which are related to, or associated with them. A thesaurus, dictionary of idioms, *Brewers Phrase and Fable* or other books can help, or you can use one or more of the following structured brainstorming techniques.

## People, places, props

For this we draw up three columns headed as above and write whatever comes into the head. Then, we try to find a connection between anything listed in one column and something listed in either of the other columns. From the lists below ideas could be sparked for sketches with Father Christmas trying to deliver a piano to a lighthouse; a ghost which haunts a fridge; a drunkard losing a contact lens under the sofa.

Some ideas may be stronger than others, some may have to be rejected as being too extreme or fanciful. The main aim is to get your brain ticking over and once you have found many connections, you will be able to select those which have the most potential for further development.

| People | Places | Props |
|---|---|---|
| Doctor | Cake shop | Sun glasses |
| Lawyer | Bus | Piano |
| Father Christmas | Aquarium | Window |
| Baby | Travel agency | Fridge |
| Mother | Ballroom | Coffee |
| Ghost | Lighthouse | Contact lens |
| Drunkard | Under the sofa | Horseshoe |
| Student | Bar | Spoon |

## Mind webbing (aka spiders)

This involves a stream of consciousness and free association of ideas. You can then select whichever associations fit best. Starting from the idea that

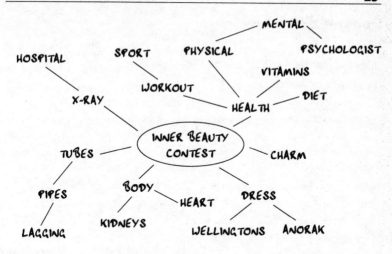

**Figure 3.1    Mind webbing**

inner beauty may mean more than outer beauty, what if there were to be inner beauty contests?

Using the associations in Figure 3.1 as the basis for a sketch, we could follow a former 'Ms/Mr Cute Kidneys' as x-rays are produced, interviews with a psychologist are undertaken, and so on.

## Six honest serving men

> I keep six honest serving men, (They taught me all I knew): Their names are What and Why and When, And How and Where and Who.
>
> Rudyard Kipling, 'The Elephant's Child' in *Just So Stories*

For this technique, you would draw up six columns headed, 'What', 'Why', 'When', 'How', 'Where', and 'Who', and write associations in the appropriate columns. You would then look for connections in the same way as for people, places and props. You may find this method useful for brainstorming on political subjects or taboo topics for example.

## Doing it differently

For this we draw up two columns. In one we write an ordinary format, and in the second we write a different way of doing it.

| Ordinary format | Different format |
| --- | --- |
| Court case | Nursery rhyme characters on trial |
| News bulletins | Read by toddlers/aliens |
| | As a rap/in verse/Shakespearean language |
| Football commentary | Tiddlywinks commentary |
| Road traffic report | Supermarket traffic report |

In the next chapter we will look at the rules and techniques of comedy writing and you may find these will help with generating ideas too.

---

**EXERCISES**

**1** Obtain recordings or printed copies of 20 sketches and ascertain the premise of each. You should be able to do this in a few words.

**2** Using any of the idea generating techniques, think of premises for ten sketches.

# 4 | COMEDY WRITING TECHNIQUES

No matter what the form of comedy, the essential craft of comedy writing involves the understanding and skilful use of the same rules and techniques. Develop your craft skills successfully, and you will gain the flexibility needed to write for the wide range of outlets for comedy material.

First, we must make the distinction between rules and techniques. Techniques are the basic tools which can be used to shape and fashion the wood of comedy, whereas rules are inflexible and have to obeyed.

## Golden rules of comedy

### 1 It must be economical

Being too wordy or going off at a tangent will diminish the effectiveness of your funnies and your audience will probably be stony faced. If you think of your funny as a journey, then an audience will want to know no more than the departure point (establishing the funny), the route (the body of the funny), and when they have arrived (the punchline). This is not to say you can't take the scenic route through the body of the funny, however you should make frequent stops at several stations where there should be punchlines to keep the journey interesting.

Cutting out anything which does not contribute to the joke, and writing tight, well-structured funnies, will prevent your audience getting lost on their journey. But don't be so economical as to make the journey a mystery tour with only clues to what the joke is about. Let it run at its natural pace, but without the diversions and dead ends.

### 2 It must be self explanatory

Any funny can be said to have failed if it has to be explained. There are a number of reasons for the failure of something that you thought was funny but which leaves an audience saying, 'I don't get it.'

If a funny is not getting laughs, perhaps it is using an obscure allusion or reference, or is an 'in' joke of relevance only to certain people 'in' the know. Perhaps the situation and character or the reason underlying the premise of the funny is illogical or unclear. Always aim for clarity and a clearly defined target and point to a joke.

## 3 It must be funny

It might seem obvious to say comedy has to be funny, but it is surprising how often this can be forgotten. Given the subjective nature of comedy, there are never going to be any clear labels saying, 'This is funny', and neither is it possible to make all the people laugh all the time. Nevertheless, a comedy writer does have to make somebody laugh, somewhere, not just sometimes but with great regularity.

There is no room for self indulgence in comedy and the final authority on whether something is funny is always going to be the audience. With that in mind, comedy that has a good, strong, original premise, is well written and well targeted, will have the right fertilizer and growing conditions for laughter.

# Comedy techniques

## Exaggeration

This is a commonly used technique which includes hyperbole, distortion and overstatement. Simply, it may be a straightforward exaggeration – a man says he is only going into a pub for one drink, when we next see him, that one drink is in a glass of gigantic proportions.

The exaggeration may also be used in the form of a simile or metaphor, for example, 'The house was so small that ...' or 'I wouldn't say he was extravagant but ...', with the punchline being some exaggeration of the adverb.

Exaggeration can also be set in the context of situation and character:

> A friend of mine doesn't like spending money so you can imagine my surprise when I found her surrounded by bags of wallpaper she'd been scraping off.
>
> 'Are you redecorating? It's only 20 years since you last did it.'
>
> 'I'm not decorating – I'm moving.'

The 20 years is a bit of sarcastic exaggeration, whereas the premise of taking the wallpaper when you move is an exaggeration of meanness.

When using an exaggeration technique, think about the extent of the exaggeration. Which would be funnier, to see the friend with the kind of wallpaper which pulls off in long lengths, or having her stripping wallpaper which comes off in tiny scraps?

The notion of the friend taking the wallpaper with her is only a small step from reality in that although it is unlikely anyone would do this, it's not improbable, unlike the following exaggerated situation:

> I've always been the sort of guy who'd keep his cocoa warm by burning down the orphanage.
>
> > Bob Monkhouse, speaking of the characters he has
> > played in dramatic roles

Bob Monkhouse is saying that he's not just played villains, he's played villains who are more evil and meaner than most. An exaggerated menace is achieved by juxtaposing cocoa, which has associations of warm, happy cosiness, with an orphanage, which has associations of coldness and sadness for lonely and innocent children.

You will always find that the greater the exaggeration, the more unrealistic and improbable the situation becomes. An audience will then not be able to relate to the funny, unless it is set within a fantastical or surreal world where the base level of reality is already distorted. Aim to keep the extent of the exaggeration within the boundaries of the tone and style of the comedian, show or narrative comedy you are writing for.

## Bathos and understatement

Whereas exaggeration increases the scale, bathos decreases and the big, the powerful and the grandiose, are reduced to the small, the everyday and the unimportant.

The film *Dr Strangelove; or, How I Learned to Stop Worrying and Love the Bomb* with its premise of an imminent nuclear destruction of the world which the military doesn't see as too big a deal, shows how bathos lends itself naturally to black comedy.

> I don't say we wouldn't get our hair mussed, but I do say no more than 10–20 million people will be killed.

The *non sequitur*, of which Woody Allen is an angst-ridden master, also lends itself well to bathos.

> And my parents finally realized that I'm kidnapped and they snap into action immediately: They rent out my room.
>
> Woody Allen

The kidnapping of a child is an event of major proportions and the anecdotal funny could have gone straight from the realization of the kidnapping, to renting out the room. By saying 'they snap into action immediately' the situation is made to sound much more dramatic, it has reached greater heights, which then makes for a more effective ending.

If you think of a bathos technique as being a skier ascending a mountain, then the higher the skier goes, the greater the exhilaration and fun in the descent. Always look to see if you can take the situation higher, but don't climb so high that the skier goes past the mountain top into outer space. Keep within the realms of reality and credibility of the premise created.

Both exaggeration and bathos techniques can be used to great effect in spoofs and parodies, where there is exaggeration or understatement of key characteristics of a genre, situation or person.

Satire, too, will often use these same technique to highlight the deficiency of the government or other organization, bureaucracy or personalities to get a particular point across.

## Absurdity

> A friend of mine was told he was too young to join the army, so he lied about his species, and joined a horse regiment.
>
> Hovis Presley

Absurdity is a ridiculous, ludicrous, non-sensical and illogical view of the world. It plays around with the ordinary and the extraordinary, is always imaginative and has a high visual content.

Absurdity can be quite logical in realistic situations:

- Sue Townsend's Adrian Mole character sitting in a hospital A & E department with a model aeroplane stuck to his nose after a glue sniffing experiment.
- Victoria Wood talking of train journeys in which she always ends up 'sitting next to the woman who's eating an

individual fruit pie by sucking the filling through the hole in the middle.'

Absurdity can also be extremely logical in unrealistic situations:

How do you know if an elephant's been in the refrigerator? There are footprints in the butter.

Once you accept the situation in this children's joke – that elephants can get into the refrigerator, it is quite logical and expected to find footprints in the butter.

This does seem to go against the idea that punchlines should be unexpected. The humour in elephant jokes, however, comes from the ridiculous visual images conjured up, and from the listener realizing they've been tricked into accepting the distorted reality.

## Incongruity

Humour results from the contrast between a thing as it is and ought to be, and a thing smashed out of shape, as it ought not to be.

Stephen Leacock

As human beings we have certain expectations as to the nature and normality of the world we live in. Incongruity twists that idea around and gains humour from placing together character, or story elements, which don't usually go together.

For example, incongruity in a sketch from *The Million Pound Radio Show* by Nick Revell and Andy Hamilton put together olden day pirates and modern day employment practices, and had the pirates demanding training days and a crèche.

## Contrast

The basic premise of contrast is that of 'odd couples' – unlikely pairings and opposites, while not funny in themselves, become so when put together.

In the film *Twins*, Arnold Schwarzenegger is a big man but his size in itself is not funny. Neither is the smallness of Danny de Vito. Put them side by side, however, even better, use incongruity and make them twins, and suddenly big and small becomes even bigger and smaller.

The 'odd couple' notion is used to great effect in the Neil Simon play, film and TV series of that name, in which enormous fun is gained from the relationship between the apartment sharing obsessively houseproud Felix and the relaxed and slobby Oscar.

## Irony

> **irony**. *n*. covert ridicule which exposes the faults or follies of others by an assumed ignorance, accompanied by an implied conscious superiority, of, what is the true state of affairs.'
>
> *Collins New English Dictionary*

Dramatic irony, when an audience knows something the characters in the drama do not, is perhaps the easiest form of irony to understand. Comedic irony however, is a bit more subtle and difficult to master, as it relies on an audience understanding the subtext or duality of the meaning in a funny. Often comic irony will rely on what is implied, rather than stated.

> When I said I wanted to be a comedian everyone laughed at me, well, they're not laughing now.
>
> Bob Monkhouse

There is irony here in the dual meaning of the word laughter – it can be the laughter of ridicule, or the laughter of response to a gag. One is a negative statement, the other a positive. As Bob Monkhouse is a very successful comedian with over 40 years of successful mirth making, there is an even greater irony.

## The outrageous

> My dear fellow, I never saw anything so funny in my life, and yet it was not in the least bit vulgar.
>
> W S Gilbert, humorist and lyricist

Use this technique carefully! Be too outrageous, shocking, repulsive, disrespectful or irreverent, and you will do no more than offend or embarrass. The British 'Carry On' films were certainly outrageous in their sauciness and use of innuendo, but got the balance right, in that they were never crude or indecent.

The outrageous may be no more than an extreme and outlandish way of dressing (Dame Edna Everidge), an outspoken style of comedy (Ruby Wax), or a challenge to widely accepted opinion, for example Dennis Leary, whose stand-up act positively promotes smoking.

Controversial topics, religion, sex and politics will always provide plenty of opportunity to be outrageous, as will challenges to the status quo and anything which is cherished or regarded highly by society as a whole. Remember the golden rule which says comedy should be funny, and aim for being funny rather than being shocking just for the hell of it.

There are restrictions on how outrageous comedy material can be – broadcast regulations have regard for taste and decency while, for example, the British Board of Film Classification can withhold a license from films considered depraving, corrupting or greatly and gratuitously offensive.

Live performances on the other hand have very few restrictions. Aggressive humour, 'in-your-face' humour, bad language and risqué material have all found their place in live venues, but will always carry the risk of not being acceptable to an audience. (See also Chapter 13, Stand-up comedy – Material and the audience.)

## Misunderstanding

A misunderstanding may lead a character into doing, or saying, something which then causes complications of comic proportions. Farce is a form of comedy which makes extensive use of misunderstandings. There are several ways of using this technique, for example misunderstandings generated between characters and situations within the joke. This may be:

■ **Intentional**

*Boss*  Have you prepared the redundancy notices for all the shirkers?

*Employee*  Yes, and here's yours.

■ **Unintentional**

*Teacher*  You're full of beans today, Johnny!

*Johnny*  How did you know what I had for lunch, Miss?

The misunderstanding arises because Johnny, not having a firm grasp of language and phraseology, takes the phrase 'full of beans' literally. The variety of expressions used by different generations, cultures, classes, nationalities and also technical and professional jargon, all provide many opportunities for misunderstandings.

## The mislead

A variation on misunderstanding is to mislead the audience by using the expectations which accompany the use of familiar expressions and formats.

### Familiar expressions or phrases

Local police were indebted today when they acted on information received – and it fell at the first fence.

By using police jargon such as 'information received' in the set-up to the above funny we are led to believe it is about crime and criminals. The punchline, however, tells us that this is information of a different kind, a racing tip. We have been misled.

### Familiar format

The film *Jaws* and the theme associated with the approach of a shark is so well known that we would only need to see a frightened face, hear the theme and a sinister voice saying, 'Just when you thought it was safe to go back into the water …' and we would instantly think 'shark'.

Playing around with these expectations we can lead the audience to expect one thing, then give them something else. For example we could say, 'Just when you thought it was safe to go into the water again' and then give the unexpected punchline of, 'they let another school party in' and show a swimming pool with hordes of children pouring in. Note how the punchline uses exaggeration by associating the terrors of man-eating sharks and children.

## Innuendo and double entendre

The marvellous thing about a joke with a double meaning is that it can only mean one thing.

Ronnie Barker

The substance of innuendo and double entendre are words with double meanings, euphemisms and subtle and oblique ways of referring to, usually, something sexual. It is a joke which relies entirely on the imagination of the audience in understanding what is being referred to.

*Hacker*   I hit two beautiful balls today.
*Caddy*   The only way you could do that, sir, would be to step on a rake.

Melvin Helitzer

Sauciness is often more acceptable than anything verging on the pornographic, so do be aware of the boundaries of good and bad taste, keep the intended audience in mind, and if writing for TV, remember that shows broadcast before 9p.m. should be suitable for children to watch.

## The put-down

> From the moment I picked up your book until I laid it down I was convulsed with laughter. Someday I intend reading it.
>
> Groucho Marx

We all like to see the deflation of the pompous and pretentious but for a put-down joke to work it has to be deserved.

We quite rightly laugh when an arrogant and conceited person walks into a lamp post, or has a drink thrown over him when he has been lecherous at the bar. However, if there is no element of truth or the humour strays into hurt, the joke has probably gone too far.

Satire often makes use of the put-down to deflate and expose inadequacies in the working of government, while the stand-up comedian will have a stock of witty one-line put-downs for use against hecklers.

## Word plays

Word plays do not often have visual imagery and are often more clever than funny. They are not in favour so much today, unless they are very good, and should never be used for foreign language markets as they will be impossible to translate effectively.

## Puns

Often the most disparaged of word plays, puns use words similar in sound, but different in sense. They are a way of playing around with words which is often used in children's jokes of the question and answer kind:

*Q* What noise does a grape make when you crush it?
*A* It just gives a little whine.

## Twisted cliché

Here, a familiar phrase or expression is given a different ending, or words are changed to make the cliché more appropriate.

If all the cars on the road were laid end to end … it would be a Bank Holiday.

The twisting of a familiar form of new reporting can also be twisted.

A fire was put out at the Tax Office before any serious good was done.

## Grammatical distortion

> If the baby doesn't like cold milk, boil it.
> Quoted in Gyles Brandreth, *Joke Box*

When the subject and object of a sentence become confused, inadvertently humorous sayings can result.

There are also forms of grammatical inaccuracy which take their names from particular individuals.

## Malapropism

These derive from the character Mrs Malaprop in Sheridan's *The Rivals* and are the misuse of sound alike words. Malapropisms create a bizarre world in which bosses exterminate their employees' services, athletes perspire to be Olympic champions and an old man is likely to talk of having his boils blanched. The misused word should enhance, and say something amusing, telling or satirical.

## Goldwynism

Movie maker Sam Goldwyn lends his name to grammatical mistakes which give the malaprop another twist. Classic Goldwynisms are, 'If I want your opinion, I'll tell it to you,' and, 'A verbal contract isn't worth the paper it is written on.'

## Colemanball

Colemanballs gain their name from British television sports presenter, David Coleman, whose capacity for making illogical comments led to a column in the satirical magazine *Private Eye* being named after him. They are the unthinking and contradictory statements and slips of the tongue made by pressured presenters whose mouths often work faster than their brains:

That's the fastest time ever run – but it's not as fast as the world record.

David Coleman

The Americans' heads are on their chins a little bit at the moment.

Ron Pickering

## Spoonerism

Reverend W A Spooner gives his name to the transposing of initial letters of key words:

You have hissed all my mystery lectures.

The Spoonerism which has an underlying truth to the misuse will work best.

# Structural techniques

## The rule of three

For some unknown reason, in the comedy world threes seem to work best – things are bad, they get worse, then they get taxed; things are good, they get better, then you get a job as a taxman. The three should always have an increasing, or decreasing sequence.

## The delay

Just when you thought something was going to be funny, it isn't, then it is.

Delaying the punchline gives the thrill of anticipation:

We see a woman walking carefully along with a tray of eggs, a potted plant is about to drop from a window ledge – the expected doesn't happen – a shop awning is pulled out and catches the pot.

We see an awning pole swing towards the eggs as the man holding it dives to catch the pot as it plunges through the awning – again the expected doesn't happen – the pole catches on something at the last minute.

Then the woman trips and breaks the eggs.

Note how this joke follows the rule of three with the eggs being broken in an unexpected way after two near misses. Would it have been effective had there been fewer mishaps, or more?

## The twist reverse

A twist in the normal expectation of the way things happen can give a sense of satisfied justice, and often surreal events. If shooting gallery ducks turn around and shoot at people, or an advertisement shows hedgehogs moving along the road and leaving a trail of flattened cars in their wake, twist reverses have been used.

Taking the point of view set up at the beginning of a joke and twist reversing so it unexpectedly cancels itself out, is another way of using the technique.

> Goldie Hawn is funny, sexy, beautiful, talented, intelligent, warm and consistently sunny. Other than that, she doesn't impress me at all.
>
> Neil Simon

## The topper

Topping a joke with another one which unexpectedly springs from the original is a good way of extending a joke.

In a Hale and Pace sketch we see Norman out jogging: when he comes to a road he has to stop for traffic. Tired of waiting to cross the road, he pushes another jogger in front of a car to stop the traffic. That's the joke. It was topped when a concerned Gareth got out of the car with a first-aid box. Then, ignoring the injured jogger, he took a paint tin from the first-aid box and attended to the scratch on his car. Note how a mislead technique is used to top the joke – the first-aid box was intended to make us believe any concern was for the jogger.

## The running gag

A running gag is a joke which is repeated throughout a show or film and has the same familiarity that a catch phrase has.

The Neil Simon film *The Out of Towners* makes use of the running gag with the phrase, 'Oh, my God,' which the wife repeats in a flat resigned way whenever another thing in the City of New York conspires against them.

Once we know the phrase signals impending disaster, we do not need to see the attack, robbery or whatever and can cut to the effects afterwards. A neat way of moving the film on and keeping the pace up.

The same film also uses a running gag of characterization, with the husband constantly writing down the names of everyone, including a dog, who annoys them, with the intention of taking legal action.

# Specialized modes of comedy

## Satire

> A work in which vices, follies, stupidities, abuses, etc, are held up to ridicule and contempt.
>
> *Webster*

Satire is comedy with a serious aim of having something to say on well-defined targets, usually politics, human foolishness and weakness.

It is comedy with an edge that can wound, undermine institutions and expose the pretences of individuals in the public eye. Satire must therefore have a high degree of truth and keep on the right side of the laws of defamation, slander and libel.

Satire should always have an emphasis on humour and not be a lecture or self-opinionated tirade which could well alienate an audience. The subject matter also needs to be familiar to an audience.

## Parody

Particularly useful for sketches, parody is an exaggerated imitation of somebody or something. The distinguishing features of whatever is being parodied should first be identified, and then exaggerated.

For a parody of the TV soap format for instance, we might list: a higher rate of disasters and extra marital affairs; lots of gossiping neighbours talking to each other more than they would do in real life; nobody gets pregnant except by accident or IV treatment, and so on.

Once the elements or reference points have been identified, these then become the basis for comic interpretation.

## Slapstick

Slapstick is a boisterous form of comedy relying on the knockabout and physical humour – clowning, Punch and Judy shows, custard pies in the face, walking into doors and lamp posts, falling out of windows, and so on. It should be playful and harmless.

Slapstick is a purely visual comedy and a script may not always be used. For slapstick which also tells a story, for example, cartoons, the Mr Bean TV series and film, a script would be a narrative of the action, events and misadventures.

Is it difficult to sustain slapstick for a lengthy period without a narrative strand but slapstick sequences can be used for sketches, or included in longer comedy works. Pantomime, for instance, always has a good splattering of slapstick routines.

## Combining the techniques

These rules and techniques will give a good grounding for writing any form of comedy. You can also put your own stamp of originality, inventiveness and creativity onto them.

Think also of how the different techniques can be combined, as in the following description of a television advertisement for Boddington's beer.

We see an elegant and sophisticated looking couple (the set-up for a mislead technique). The woman slaps the creamy head of a pint of beer on her face (an exaggeration). The man then complements her, speaking with a North of Britain accent – 'By heck, you smell great.' (Reverse twist.) In brackets are the techniques used to create an incongruous situation.

---

**EXERCISES**

**1** Collect together 20 one-line gags which have either been published, broadcast or used by comedians. Analyse the techniques used to gain the joke.

**2** Make a transcript of several radio or television sketches and analyse the comedy techniques used.

---

# 5 | ONE-LINERS

Learning to write one-liners (aka lines, jokes, packaged jokes) is learning about basic joke structures, from which you will gain an understanding of comic timing and pace.

Not only are one-liners useful moneyspinners in their own right, because they encapsulate a single funny idea, they can be looked upon as the building bricks from which sketches, anecdotes, articles and other comedy material can be constructed.

The term one-liner is not entirely accurate as some one-liners are composed of several lines: essentially they are a short succinct joke with a single idea or target.

## Thought required

The best one-liners are those which cause you to think:

I go for a swim every single day. It's either that or buy a new golf ball.

Bob Hope

In this example we have to think about the connection between going for a swim and golf balls. The basic premise is that of a man who is very mean, and a very bad golf player in that he is always losing his ball, or would be if it wasn't for that swim.

You should not have to think too hard, however. A line which runs, 'If a joke loses its rhythm, there'll be a pregnant pause,' may be understood by a Catholic, who recognizes the word-play connection between the rhythm method of birth control and pregnancy, but perhaps others would not. Remember, one of the three golden rules of comedy is that it should be self explanatory.

# Visual imagery

The best one-liners also have strong visual imagery. Prince Charles's large
ears have been a comic target for a long while so it is easy to visualize the
picture in the following line:

> Can you imagine if Prince Charles became king? His ears would
> never fit on the stamps.
>
>                                                          John Martin

# Construction of one-liners

The usual construction is to have a feed (non funny) line (aka straight
line, set-up) as when Oscar Wilde says, 'To lose one parent Mr
Worthington, may be regarded as a misfortune ...' followed by a
punchline (aka tag, pay off) which should be funny ... 'to lose both, looks
like carelessness.'

> A good set-up seduces the audience into listening to you. A good
> punch forces them to react.
>
>                                                          Judy Carter

## Feed lines

Feed lines should set up the idea in one-liners quickly and succinctly, and
in the minimum number of words. Here are some examples of how you
can establish a feed line:

- a question – 'Did you know that ...'
- a statement – 'Laughter can bring tears to the eyes ...'
- an observation – 'Have you ever noticed how ...'
- a historical fact – 'Ancient Egyptian pyramid builders used
  to drink beer morning, noon and night ...'
- a news item – 'Unemployment figures have fallen again
  this month ...'

## Punchlines

A punchline rounds the joke off and should result in laughter. Punchlines
should have an unexpected twist or viewpoint and should relate to the feed
line. If you have trouble finding a punchline for a gag, use the idea
generating techniques discussed in Chapter 3.

One-liners are usually structured so there is a comma, some kind of pause or a full stop just before the punchline. This structural rhythm is implicitly understood by most people and predisposes them to expect a punchline they can laugh at. Sometimes, it is understood so well, like Pavlov's dogs, people will laugh, even if the joke is not very funny.

Let's look at how not to write a one-liner:

> Scientists are always messing about. I think they get paid far too much money myself and too much money is being wasted on those cloning experiments. If they ever did it with humans who knows where it'd end? We could get lots of tax inspectors and thousands of people all looking the same and I wouldn't fancy it if there were lots of men looking like my Dad. He's really ugly.

There are numerous faults in the joke – we don't know what it's about, it's too wordy, it doesn't start at the right point, the punchline doesn't have any punch and is lost somewhere in the middle, and the whole thing lacks rhythm and punctuation. Let's see now if we can knock it into shape.

The first thing to do is define the premise of the (would-be) joke. In this case it is trying to say something about a human cloning experiment producing too many tax inspectors.

We should then underline all the essential words needed to get this idea across. They are: cloning experiment – humans – tax inspectors. All the joke teller's opinions about scientists and her Dad, whom we do not know, are not relevant.

Separating the essential words should show a single causal connection and crystallize the basic idea. If they don't, you may need to rethink your basic idea. Remember – one target/idea per one-liner.

Once you have the essential words, all that needs to be done is to add the words for the joke to make sense grammatically and for the idea to come across clearly and instantly. A second draft of the joke might read:

> A human cloning experiment has produced a lot of tax inspectors.

This has all the essential information, but it is flat and sounds more like a feed line waiting for a punchline. There is no emotion in the joke so let's try adding a few words:

> Medical research suffered a setback today when a human cloning experiment went terribly wrong, and produced thousands of tax inspectors.

The joke is now in the form of a spoof news item and the language would need to be adjusted if it were to be used in a stand-up set or some other form.

## Make every word count

If a word doesn't add to the joke, or help it make sense, it should be taken out. Rewrite jokes until you have the best words with the biggest impact. Always ask, 'Is there a better word or phrase I could use?'

## Emphases

The emphases in a one-liner can make it or break it. A sentence has its strongest emphasis at the end, so the relevant word or idea that is going to make a joke work has to come as near to that point as sense will allow. If you remember that you want an audience to laugh at the end of the joke, not the middle, then you cannot go far wrong.

The second strongest emphasis is at the beginning of a sentence. Notice the difference between, 'Susan, will you pass the pencil,' and 'Will you pass the pencil, Susan?'

The right emphases and the right punctuation give the right rhythm and pace for good comic timing.

## Punctuation

If commas, full stops and pauses are not indicated properly, a joke could come out totally different, or be lost altogether.

> 'Mind if I join you?'
> 'Why? Am I coming apart?'
> Groucho Marx

Looking at the above, consider whether the reply would have had the same effect if it had been written, 'Why am I coming apart?'

Read your one-liners out aloud, or record them, and then listen to where the pauses and emphases are. If possible, get someone else to read them to you, and listen carefully.

# Switching

It is a bad idea to steal other people's one-liners or to dig out your own old jokes and re-use them. However, they can be 'switched' to create new jokes from the basic elements of another joke. There are four ways of doing this:

- ■ *Switch the feed line* The cloning/tax inspector one-liner could be switched as follows: 'A new government scheme is forcing the unemployed to take demeaning jobs – that's why there are so many tax inspectors.'
- ■ *Switch the punchline* Using the same one-liner, some other category of hated or disliked individual or group of people could be substituted, for example real estate agents, theatre critics or traffic wardens. The gag could be personalized for certain audiences or use a topical reference.
- ■ *Parallel the gag* A cartoon which shows a headstone with a funny inscription could be switched to show either cartoon or TV clips of office doors with funny inscriptions.
- ■ *Build on the premise* For this you would switch the premise of a joke to another situation, character or location.

My sister's a genius in the kitchen. She can have a three-course dinner for 18 people ready in less than five minutes – she just phones for a take-away.

This joke has the premise of either laziness or inventiveness, depending on your viewpoint, which could lead to thinking of other ways of showing these attributes. The joke could also possibly be switched to a TV quickie. (See also Chapter 8, Television – Layout.)

Once you understand how to construct one-liners you will find there are many ways in which the same skills can be used in different market outlets.

# Gag sheets

Gag sheets are a page or pages of one-liners. They may be on mixed topics, or on a particular theme, for example, sport, topical, risqué, dogs, holidays. Gag sheets can be advertised for sale in trade newspapers and magazines.

Buyers of gag sheets include comedians, radio and club disc jockeys, TV game show hosts, after dinner and other speakers, those giving presentations, or indeed anyone who needs to speak, perform, or persuade in an entertaining way.

Alternatively, you may be asked to write more personalized sheets. You would then need to advertise 'jokes written to order' and charge a higher fee.

## Stand-up comedians

As people whose job is to tell jokes on a regular basis, stand-up comedians may be big purchasers of gag sheets, adapting the jokes to their own style and delivery. If this is done with skill, the joke should become unique and original to each comedian who tells it.

With an emphasis today being very much on a comedian having original material many may want to solicit or consider jokes and routines direct from writers. (See also Chapter 13, Stand-up comedy.)

# Joke books

There are many jokes books on the market for both children and adults. Children's joke books generally have a variety of jokes while adult books may be themed – Jewish jokes, rugby jokes, lawyer jokes, for example. There is no reason why you cannot compile similar books: anything which is an original concept and is, of course, good will have a fighting chance of being accepted by a publisher.

You will need to send a proposal together with several pages indicating the kind of thing you intend to fill the book with. If you have any comedy experience or publication credits, indicate this in a covering letter or in the form of a curriculum vitae (aka Résumé).

You can find a publisher by using market reference books, or looking through your local library or bookshop to see who publishes similar kinds of books.

# Speeches

While some speakers may purchase gag sheets there is also a market for writers of complete speeches consisting of one-liners, humorous anecdotes and material specific to the speaker's audience.

You will need to know the kind of function the speaker will be attending and who is likely to be there. This is one place where 'in' jokes will find their niche.

The structure of a speech is a narrative of linked jokes and anecdotes which have a logical order and build towards the end, when there should be a good strong rousing funny.

You could offer your services as a speech writer by advertising in newspapers, trade and business journals or ask companies to display your details on their notice boards.

## Greetings cards

There is a growing market for humorous greetings cards and writing jokes for this outlet follows similar principles to writing one-liners. There is more detailed information in Chapter 14, Cartoon and comic strip, greetings cards.

## Competition slogans and tiebreakers

> If you can make them laugh, you're halfway there.
> Rita Smallburn, (regular competitions entrant)

This may seem an odd thing for a comedy writer to consider but what is a slogan or tiebreaker but a concise one-liner?

You will most likely be given the equivalent of a straight line such as, 'My dog eats Greedyguts dog food because …' and then you will have to supply the equivalent of a punchline in a maximum number of words.

Research the product, reading advertising features and other material to ascertain what the manufacturers think are the product's assets. Make your punchline say something about the product which is both positive and has a humorous twist and you will have the advantage over some banal and badly targeted statement. You may find puns and other word plays which have a touch of cleverness will work very well in this context of competition slogans.

For some competitions humour will not be appreciated – cosmetics, for instance, should not be joked about, but if the entry form is witty and has lots of exclamation marks, it is a good bet that humour will be appreciated.

# Copywriting

This follows on from slogans in that publicists, advertisers and promoters may need people to come up with sharp, snappy copy about their products or services.

Copywriting is a job in itself and advertising agencies usually employ creative people so there may not be so many opportunities.

Some small companies, however, do not have the financial resources to use advertising agencies and may be more willing to consider ideas, phrases and slogans on an ad hoc basis.

# Radio

There may be radio programmes which accept one-liners and you should write to the Light Entertainment Manager requesting information on upcoming shows and a writer's brief, if available. (See also Chapter 7, Radio.)

# Television

Despite funnies seeming to flow spontaneously from the mouths of presenters, this is not always so, and game and panel show presenters, topical comedy shows and others may be in the market for one-liners.

> That's our job. To make it seem that what we've written has just come out of their mouths.
>
> > John O'Farrell, comedy writer with
> > 'Clive Anderson Talks Back' and
> > 'They Think it's All Over'

As a comedy writer you will need to get into the habit of watching the end credits of shows in which anybody uses funny lines. The writers mentioned may be commissioned writers but these don't just fall out of the sky, they have to be found.

If there is a particular show or presenter you think you could write for, you could send off samples of your work together with a list of your comedy credits (if applicable).

As shows are often recorded many months before broadcast you will need to research when a new series may be coming up. Write to the production company or broadcaster of the show for information.

## Spot cartoons

You may be able to interest an artist in drawing up your one-liners as spot cartoons – single frame cartoons. Often the picture will act as the equivalent of a feed line while the caption will be the punchline, although there are variations. (See also Chapter 14, Cartoon and comic strip, greetings cards.)

## Magazine and other publications

Reader's Digest, with its fabulous payment rates, uses fillers of various descriptions which can be adapted from one-liners. You may find other magazines which may be interested and also newspapers may use them.

Research is the key word to finding outlets in this area. Use market reference books and browse the newsagents' shelves.

---

**EXERCISES**

**1** Using ten of the one-liners you collected for study in Chapter 4, switch them to write ten jokes of your own.

**2** Write five one-liners on a subject you know quite a lot about.

**3** Write five one-liners on a subject you know little about. (This will involve a bit of research but will stretch your abilities.)

---

# 6 | SKETCHES

This chapter identifies the general points about sketch writing, while the following two chapters deal more specifically with writing sketches for radio and television.

Having material used by a comedy sketch show (aka broken comedy show) can bring you a radio or television credit and may be a tool to open other doors. Getting your work shown in this way is not as difficult as imagined. While shows usually have a core of commissioned writers who are under contract to supply material, many shows are also open to unsolicited material.

## So, what is a comedy sketch?

Definitions vary, but generally a sketch is considered to be a funny scene, complete in itself, which will have a running time of a maximum of one to three minutes. Very short sketches, sometimes lasting as few as 15 seconds, are known as quickies and may be no more than an extended one-liner or visual joke.

A sketch will have a single, clearly defined premise, several verbal and/or visual jokes which evolve from the character or situation within the premise, and will end with a punchline which is both logical and unexpected.

### The writer's brief

Many shows which actively encourage sketch submissions will have a writer's brief. It may be just a few scribbled notes from the producer to inspire the writer, or give detailed information on studio sets and exterior locations, regular and new characterizations, deadlines and contact information. The latter may seem more useful but the scribbled note gives insight into the producer's mind, so should be thought equally valuable.

You do not have to stick religiously to a writer's brief, there is usually room for original ideas but they should fit within the parameters of the show's style and tone.

As all the writers will have the same brief you are going to have a better chance of acceptance if your sketch has the more original angle, or uses a set or location in a unique way. (See also Chapter 3, Beginning comedy writing – Generating ideas.)

## Sketch premises

The premise of a sketch should be strong, clear, and funny in itself. If you cannot say what a sketch is about in a few words, then perhaps the premise is not focused clearly enough.

Sketches such as Arthur Macrae's, 'No Ball', in which Cinderella doesn't want to go the ball (incongruity technique) or a series of Ken Dodd 'Clown Court' sketches which put nursery rhyme characters on trial (absurdity technique) have premises with immediate appeal. It is here you will appreciate how a one-liner which encapsulates a single idea may perhaps be expanded on.

Having a strong premise will be important if you should ever get the opportunity to pitch ideas to a producer or script editor. Being able to do this and get feedback on whether an idea is of interest or duplicates something already received, can save a lot of work.

## Sketch unity

As the premise of a sketch is its central core, it is important to have a unity of idea in that premise. Think of a sketch as akin to a short story, which will not work so well if it wanders off the point and loses its thread.

# Structure

## Beginnings

As a sketch is so short you cannot waste time explaining what it is about. Sketches have to set up quickly and establish the who, what, when, and where of the premise in the first few lines.

The Cinderella sketch mentioned earlier has stage instructions describing the scene as the curtain rises and we would see Cinderella, dressed contemporarily, while a bemused Fairy Godmother looks on. The audience can immediately see who the characters are, and the dialogue sets up the comic incongruity in the premise immediately.

> CINDERELLA: (STOPPING HER WORK FOR A MOMENT)
> Look! I may as well be frank. I don't want to go
> to the ball.
>
> Arthur Macrae – 'No Ball'

Where possible begin your sketch in the midst of action, or use an establishing device relevant to the medium the sketch is intended for. (See also Chapter 7, Radio – Setting up a radio sketch.)

## Middles

The body of a sketch should fulfil the potential of the premise, be consistent in tone and style, and keep an audience interested and entertained with funnies.

The shortness of sketches dictates that there is no room for reflective thought or elaborate subtleties. Let the characters and situation generate the jokes and make full use of the potentials of the medium you are writing for.

## Endings

When your sketch has run its course, stop. Anything which comes after a punchline will only be an anticlimax. It will also be drowned by laughter.

## Titles

Titles for sketches should give some suggestion as to the premise of the sketch, without giving the punchline away. If you can make a title interesting, intriguing or funny, so much the better. The following titles all have something intriguing about them:

> 'A Job Only Fit For Humans' by Wil Walker.
> 'Mister Grumpy' by John Brown.
> 'Late Home Parents' by Melvyn Dover.
> 'Three Paper Rounds' by Andrew Hastings.

If you have several sketches on the same theme, or in the same location don't give them generic titles such as 'Garden of Eden – 1', 'Garden of Eden – 2'. Not only may someone have sketches with the same names if you are working to a brief, but generic titles don't tell a script editor with mountains of scripts to read what your sketch is about. It is much better to have a supplementary title which gives a development of the generic situation. For example: 'Garden of Eden – Gardener wanted', Garden of Eden – Communication problems'.

# ⇨ **To market**

Current information on sketch shows looking for submissions can be found by contacting the comedy or light entertainment department of broadcasters and independent production companies.

Not all broadcasters and companies make comedy programmes so find out who does by using market reference books and making a note of companies currently broadcasting sketch shows.

With the exception of some topical shows, sketch shows are recorded ahead of broadcast, so you may need to contact the companies on a regular basis for information on current requirements.

## **Submit early**

When you do find a show looking for material, use the writer's brief, if there is one, and submit your sketches early on in the production schedules. Things are less hectic at this time: there is more chance you will be able to talk to the script editor and more chance of you being asked for a rewrite rather than getting an outright rejection. Also, if two similar sketches of the same quality are submitted, the one received first will be accepted.

Don't overload the script editor by sending too many sketches at one time. Send batches of around six sketches at intervals.

## **Bracketing sketches**

A good tactic is to submit three or four sketches for an original studio set, location or characterization, rather than just one. Any set which has to be specially made costs money and while it may not be worthwhile for one sketch, it may be for more. Similarly, bracket sketches using similar themes, topics or original formats.

## **Foreign language markets**

Sketch shows are broadcast throughout Europe and other non-English speaking countries, and you do not necessarily need to speak the language to submit material as many shows will translate English material.

Sketches which rely on word plays or colloquial expression will not translate well, so are not suitable for foreign language markets. Purely visual sketches, on the other hand, will be gladly welcomed.

If you are uncertain about the culture and everyday life in a country, for example do they have milkmen, school assemblies or Hallowe'en, try to speak to someone who knows the country or read travel books and guides, watch schools' language programmes, or get in touch with the local consulate or embassy.

Using market reference books, the Internet or joining a comedy writers' organization with links to other countries, will help with finding information on foreign broadcast companies.

## Other markets for sketches

- *Theatre*   There is very little demand for unsolicited sketches in the theatre but there are opportunities for DIY revue and sketch shows. (See also Chapter 10, Theatre – The revue; The sketch show.)
- *Copywriting, Training videos, Promotional videos*   These are specialized areas in which comedy is increasingly being used. Short sketches to illustrate points or show how things should be done, may be required.
- *DIY*   It is possible to record your own pilot show with a small group of other writers and performers. All you need is the time, a video camera or audio recording equipment, or the hire of a studio. A few shows have made it onto network TV and radio this way and cable stations are providing many other opportunities.

---

**EXERCISES**

**1** Study an existing radio sketch show, and a TV sketch show.
**2** Devise five sketch premises which will suit the radio show.
**3** Devise five sketch premises which will suit one studio set from the TV show.

---

# 7 | WRITING FOR RADIO

Although referring to sketches, this section deals with the general principles which apply to writing for radio generally.

## Advantages of writing for radio

■ *Imagination unbounded* The great beauty of radio is that anything is possible. You can locate sketches in any country, a space shuttle, under the sea or inside the head of a goldfish. With radio we can give voice to inanimate objects, hear the internal monologue of a person's thoughts, anthropomorphise animals, give voice to metaphysical, surreal and subconscious feelings and images and move through the dimensions of time and location.

■ *Lower production costs* Radio frees you from the physical and practical limitations of other mediums. You can have a cast of thousands at a football game, travel to the future or the past, and the production costs will be minimal. It can all be done with sound effects and if we look at some of the comedy sound effects in a radio library we may see there is a multitude of weird and wonderful sounds – an electric woodpecker, UFO colliding with church spire, a radiophonic stomach and a whole load of squeaky feet, twangs, creaks, bubbles and clong bong doyoyoyings, for example.

■ *Shorter production schedules* Radio shows are easier and quicker to record and do not need the long pre-production and production schedules of TV. Often the time between your material being accepted and broadcast is fairly quick, sometimes only a matter of a few days in the case of a topical show.

■ *Room for experimentation and trial* Reduced production costs make radio an ideal experimental ground in which more chances can be taken. Shows can be tested out for audience response and popularity and, if found to be successful, may transfer to TV.

■ *Greater intimacy*

The almost telepathic transference of images from mind to mind.
Martin Esslin, 'The National Theatre of the Air'

Radio has a great intimacy, speaking directly into the ear of a listener. Greater subtlety can be used and if recorded with an audience, the listener becomes part of that audience.

# The creative tools of a radio writer

Radio may not have the pictures of a visual medium, yet in creating pictures in a listener's mind, the medium is extremely powerful. So, how are these mental images created?

The tools which radio writers have at their disposal are small in number, but with skill and imagination they are big in what they can do. The tools are music, sound effects, silence and dialogue.

## Music

Music can be used to set the mood and tone for a sketch. Suspense, whimsy, nostalgia, happiness, sadness, fear – there is music to suggest, complement or parody every emotion, but remember that every extract used will entail the payment of royalties.

Music is also a useful device for establishing time and place. Lute and harpsichord music can be used to establish an Elizabethan era, and an Irish jig or the wedding march instantly set the scene. A theme tune can also usefully set up a parody of a TV soap or a game show.

Obscure recordings are best avoided and it is better not to be too specific – suggest the kind or style of music rather than a particular piece, unless that piece is essential to the humour of the sketch. If you do specify a particular piece make sure it is available as a recording.

## Sound effects (FX)

Sound effects should be used sparingly and effectively. Only put necessary sound effects in a script. If a character is making tea, for instance, there is no need to include all the individual actions, you would just put, 'FX         MAKES TEA'.

Some sound effects can be ambiguous or unrecognizable when used alone, such as skis on snow or gas hissing, so the dialogue may need, unobtrusively, to identify the sound.

Obscure or complicated sounds may be available in a sound effects library but always ask is this sound effect really necessary? Does it add to this sketch? If sketches are of equal merit the one which is simpler to record will be favoured over the one with complicated or fiddly sound effects.

There are two kinds of sound effects:

- *Background effects* which run under the dialogue and are useful for establishing place, and for giving depth and authenticity to a location. Very noisy background effects such as a battle, may drown the dialogue, so are established and then faded under the dialogue.

- *Spot effects* are a single sound and may come from a sound effects table. It is much easier, quicker and more naturalistic for someone to ring a bell, sound a horn, crumple and pop bubble wrap to give the effect of a fire, than it is to edit the sound on afterwards.

  Other spot effects which cannot be done in this way, for example, a seagull to indicate a seaside location, or a cell door slamming, will be edited on after the dialogue has been recorded.

## Silence

Under all speech that is good for anything there lies a silence that is better.

Thomas Carlyle, an essay on 'Sir Walter Scott' in
*Critical and Miscellaneous Essays*

Written as (SILENCE) in a script, a silence can be used as part of the comic timing and pace of a joke or situation. The one thing it is not, however, is empty. Consider the following kinds of silences:

- The 'no comment' silence.
- The 'I'm struggling to think of a good excuse or explanation' silence.
- The guilty silence.
- The 'I can't win without losing' dilemma.
- The 'I don't know' silence.
- The 'how can I explain this?' silence.
- The 'I'm trying to make a difficult decision ' silence.

Unless a silence is used as an ending for a sketch, in which case it will be something of a punchline, it will be significant how that silence is broken, and by whom. Silence is a very useful device in the interplay and interaction between characters.

Not silences proper, slight hesitancies, pauses and beats give pace and rhythm in a character's dialogue, and again are not empty. They should all be indicated in the script, either through punctuation or the writing of (BEAT), (PAUSE) or the use of an ellipsis. If we take the scenario of a man who is trying to impress his boss and picks up the bill in a restaurant, we could have the following exchange:

BOSS    Not too expensive, I hope.

MAN    No, not at all. (PAUSE) Oh dear. I'm sorry Mr Johnson, Fred ... I'm sorry but could you ... could you lend me ... some money (BEAT) I seem to have come out without my wallet.

SILENCE

## Dialogue

No matter what the medium, dialogue should sound realistic rather than real. It should be real life speech, but without all its meandering, asides and irrelevancies.

Any dialogue has three functions – to reveal character, move the plot forward and to convey information. As we are dealing with comedy, it also has a fourth function – to create laughs.

## Dialogue and character

A common mistake in writing any dialogue is to have all the characters speaking in the same way, usually the way the writer speaks. Characters should each have their own individualistic speech rhythms and patterns and if you cover up the names on a script, it should still be possible to determine each character. Always have honesty in dialogue and ask – would this person really say or do this in this situation?

There are many things which determine how a character speaks. Their age, class, gender, social background, education, intelligence and where they live, will all influence their speech patterns, the words they use and what they choose to talk about.

A character's personality too, will distinguish their dialogue – whether they are a bubbly, bright person, cynical, prejudiced, pessimistic, self confident, timid, arrogant or self effacing.

**Subtext** Human beings use subterfuge, avoid talking about certain topics, lie, manipulate, pretend, hide their true feelings, modify their language and use all manner of devices to prevent saying what they mean. In effect, there is always a subtext beneath the words which are actually spoken.

Know your characters well enough to understand what is going on in their heads as well as coming out of their mouths.

**Speech patterns** Giving a character a distinctive speech pattern not only individualizes their dialogue, it can serve as an identity tag. For example, a character may constantly reiterate words or phrases, always start sentences with a negative, speak ungrammatically, or use the word 'I' incessantly. Listen carefully to how people speak in real life and also listen to and read works for radio.

## Dialogue and exposition

Radio dialogue has to work harder than any other dialogue and must complement sound effects and music in establishing the physical environment and the people in it. This should be done unobtrusively and discretely, not as in Timothy West's classic parody:

> Whisky, eh? That's a strange drink for an attractive auburn-haired woman of 29 to be having.
>
> Timothy West, from *This Gun In My Right Hand Is Loaded*

If it is night, have a character talk about the stars, if it is cold, have them wish they had put their woolly vest on, if a woman is good looking, have someone describe her as a regular Liz Hurley. Find devices that sound a natural thing for the character to say in that situation, and that also move the action forward.

## Dialect and accent

**accent**    manner of pronunciation and inflection of the voice peculiar to a country, part of a country, town or individual.

**dialect**    a mode of speech peculiar in idiom, accent, vocabulary, to a district or social group; vernacular.

*Collins New English Dictionary*

You may be able to get by if you ask for the script to be read with a Liverpool, Cockney, American or Australian accent, but it will not have the unique words, sentence constructions and rhythms of the real thing. Don't use accent or dialect unless you can make it sound authentic. Research can help with getting it right or you could ask somebody who is familiar with that dialect it to check it over for you.

Dialect is best used lightly with just an occasional word or phrase to give the flavour. The meaning of unusual expressions should be apparent through the context in which they are used.

Writing accents and dialect phonetically can make a script difficult for an actor to read, so it is best to rely on sentence constructions and phraseology.

## More on dialogue

■ Use contractions – can't instead of cannot, isn't instead of is not – as this is the way people usually speak. Read your script out aloud and listen for how you are actually saying the words. Better still, record it or get a friend to read it out.

■ Dialogue has to be speakable, so avoid tongue twisters, sibilance and difficult to pronounce words.

■ Avoid empty wordage.

■ Poetic or flowery language may sound inappropriate, unless it is a particular trait in a character.

■ Short sentences work better than long rambling speeches. Don't, however, truncate speeches too much.

■ Vary the length of speeches, thinking always of the rhythm and pace.

■ Avoid ping-pong dialogue with short sharp sentences being bandied backwards and forwards, unless it is for particular effect.

■ In most verbal exchanges there is a power hierarchy. Think about who is the most dominant person in a conversation and whether this is by means of their position or personality. Think about who is leading the conversation and who is determining its content.

■ Character names may need to be used to identify the people in a sketch or scene. As we do not constantly refer to people's names in real life, the trick is to make it sound natural, for example, when calling someone, when a group of people are together and a character wants to speak to a particular person.

■ Orchestrate the various sounds of dialogue, music, sound effects and silence.

## General points

■ If there are too many characters in a scene it will not be easy for a listener to keep track of who is there.

■ Be careful you don't 'lose' characters in a scene by not having someone speak for a while. A listener will forget they are there.

■ Give characters proper entrances and exits so the listener can keep track of who is there.

■ Vary the length of sequences, the number of people speaking in scenes, the pace of the dialogue, volume of sound and locations. Sketches, on the other hand, can easily become disordered and chaotic if too much is included. The three unities of time, place and action will help sketches be more focused.

# Ways of establishing radio sketches

At the beginning of a sketch we are aiming to establish as much of the who, what, when and where of the situation as naturally and as quickly as possible.

Let's look at some examples.

### The telephone

| FX | PHONE RINGS |
|---|---|
| 1st PERSON | Hello, is that President Clinton. |

Telephones are an easy option and something of a cliché. If using this device, try to make it more original

### Recognized format

For a parody of a film, TV programme, advertisement and so on you would only need to have either the actual introductory credits (a copyright fee would have to be paid) or you could open with something of a similar style and tone that would be equally recognizable.

### Sound effects

| FX | SHIP'S HOOTER | SEA SURGING |
|---|---|---|

The ship's hooter could indicate a dockside but as there is also sea surging, which indicates a ship sailing, we can only be on a ship.

### Sound effect and dialogue

| FX | BUZZER |
|---|---|
| 1st PERSON | Next patient please! |

| FX | GAVEL BEING BANGED |
|---|---|
| 1st PERSON | Prisoner at the bar. |

In both these set-ups we know instantly where we are, who is talking and have some indication as to what the sketch is going to be about. The natural sounds and dialogue of a real situation have been used.

## ⇒ **To market**

Regional and independent radio stations are often very keen to support their listeners by using short inserts of sketches, short stories, topical jokes and to have people in to talk about their comedy writing, or do a short funny slot. On local radio however, very few of these opportunities would earn you any money.

Some network radio stations have many opportunities for sitcoms, comedy drama, original sketch shows and other comedy and light entertainment shows. There are also sketch shows which accept unsolicited scripts and the BBC's World Service opens up international opportunities. Contact details are listed in the appendices.

## Layout

Standard presentation as described in Chapter 3 should be used and Figure 7.1 shows the layout of a radio script. Other points to keep in mind are:

- Avoid carrying speeches over a page. If it is impossible to avoid splitting a speech, type (cont) at the end of a sentence and begin the next page: SUSAN (continued).
- Only give necessary instructions to actors. It should be evident how the line is to be read by its context.
- Don't use television directions for radio, such as 'sits sprawled on the settee, drinking coffee and looking at a photograph'.
- By the same token, remember gestures and facial expressions cannot be seen on radio.

The main requirement of any script is that there is clarity, and clear distinction between speech and instructions.

A page of script will equal approximately one minute of broadcast time.

1                                                     N.E. Writer
                                                      Address and phone
                                                      number on every page

SETTING OUT A RADIO SKETCH SKETCH

1.  1st PERSON      So, this is the dialogue, eh?

2.  2nd PERSON      Yes, it's double spaced and in lower case letters, unlike
                    the character speaking, that's the guy on the left, who's
                    in upper case letters. As is something like this.

3.  FX              ROAD DRILL, ESTABLISH AND FADE UNDER.

4.  1st PERSON      How'd that get in here!

5.  2nd PERSON      It's a sound effect. It's faded under so everyone can
                    still hear us speaking.

6.  1st PERSON      How do you stop it?

7.  FX              OUT

8.  2nd PERSON      Just like that! As Tommy Cooper might have said.

9.  1st PERSON      Very clever. What about music?

10. GRAMS           WHITE CHRISTMAS/BING CROSBY

11. 2nd PERSON      (VO) No problem.

12. 1st PERSON      (VO) Why hasn't it faded?

13. 2nd PERSON      (VO) Some techno whizzkid, otherwise known as the
                    technician, is fiddling about and has put us into voice
                    over, otherwise shown as (VO)

14. 1st PERSON      (VO) Just like that!

(cont)

2
N.E. Writer
Address and phone
number on every page

SETTING OUT A RADIO SKETCH SKETCH (cont)

1.  GRAMS          OUT

2.  1st PERSON     I'm getting the hang of this now!

3.  FX             PHONE RINGS

4.  1st PERSON     This will probably be a Hollywood producer. Hello.

5.  3rd PERSON     (D) This is Alphabeta windows, could I interest you …

6.  FX             PHONE SLAMMED DOWN

7.  2nd PERSON     Guess your big chance is still to come, eh?

8.  1st PERSON     OK smartypants, why did the voice sound different and
                   what are all those numbers down the side of the page?

9.  2nd PERSON     (D) tells that techno whizzkid to distort the speech so
                   it sounds as though it's coming through a phone, a
                   loudhailer, or whatever. The numbers are so everyone
                   can refer to a particular bit of the script quickly and
                   easily.

10. 1st PERSON     You've obviously done your homework but what about
                   giving every sketch a title, every page a number and
                   not running dialogue over the page?

11. 2nd PERSON     You weren't paying attention, it's already done.
                                                                    ends

**Figure 7.1    Radio script layout**

**EXERCISES**

**1** Using examples of radio sketches (published or recorded) select five which you think establish the sketch well, and for any which do this badly, see if you could establish them better.

**2** Using correct layout, describe the opening for the following radio sketch scenarios:

– a school sports day
– an in-store demonstration for beauty products
– a parody of a TV talk show

**3** Write up the sketch premises devised for radio in Chapter 6 (see page 54).

# 8 | WRITING FOR TELEVISION

This section is written with TV sketches in mind but you will find much of relevance to all TV writing.

Sketches for TV shows are generally a maximum of one to three minutes and a show may consist of all sketches, or may be mixed with one-liners and other comedy and entertainment material. Sketches may also be used to break up other types of shows, such as a David Letterman/Jack Docherty style chat show.

A sketch show may have the unity of a theme such as sport, or use only topical material. It may be star led (*The Benny Hill Show, French and Saunders, The Tracey Ullman Show*) or have a core cast (*Monty Python's Flying Circus*, the Canadian *Kids in The Hall*)

However, each show will have its own distinctive style and format which you should become familiar with if you intend to write for that show.

There is a school of thought which says writers should just write the sketches and leave their realization to the director. The sensible and more successful comedy writer, however, works to the full potential of a visual medium while also being aware of the limitations and restrictions.

## Writing visually

Always ask of any TV sketch, could this have been done anywhere else but on TV? A single facial expression or a gesture can replace something which might take several lines to convey on radio. There is also great potential for irony, with a viewer being able to see something happening behind a character's back, or suspense as a character sits on an armchair where we know incriminating evidence is hidden.

The purely visual sketch with no dialogue is always welcomed by producers but this doesn't mean that every sketch should be a mime. Think about what is being seen on screen and if you can show something, don't duplicate it in the dialogue. Words should complement and add to the pictures.

There are some things which are best avoided on TV. Given the size of a TV screen, a sketch which relies on the viewer reading a newspaper or letter would not work so well, and while the viewer is busy reading, the action is being held up.

# Camera terms

You do not need to have an extensive knowledge of TV production processes to write a script: however, it is useful to have a working knowledge of the processes, camera equipment and techniques. If you can manage it, time spent on taking a video production course or experimenting with a camcorder will be a worthwhile investment.

Camera directions should not be included in a script, unless you want to emphazise something or create a particular effect. However, it is useful to know the terms used.

- *Close-up (CU)*

  Head and shoulders, or an object fills the frame. Greater detail can be shown in a close-up, emphasis can be given to facial expression or the significance of a prop, a door handle turning, and so on.

  Close-ups are often self evident and don't need to be put in the script, such as

  SHE PICKS UP AN APPLE, WE SEE THERE IS A HUGH WORM STICKING OUT'

  There is no other way this worm could be seen without a close-up.

- *Medium or Mid shot (MS)*

  Cuts off around waist level. This is the standard shot for interviews, two shots (two people in frame) and 'talking heads'.

- *Long shot (LS)*

  A more distant shot giving information on the locality and background.

■ *Establishing shot*

This is a shot or shots used to show where we are, for example a street, office, hotel.

■ *Pan*

The camera acts as eyes following action or movement, or looking around a room. Pans are time-consuming as they need to be rehearsed and may require several takes to get right. There are also problems of keeping the camera focused and ensuring a moving object or person is always centred.

■ *Whip pan*

A fast pan. Too many can make a viewer feel dizzy.

■ *Tracking shot*

The camera is placed on dolly tracks (exterior) or wheels (studio) so it can follow moving action. Tracking does take time to rehearse and there is yet more time and expense involved in the laying of dolly tracks.

■ *Zoom*

The camera zooms in quickly to a CU.

■ *Pull focus shot*

The focus pulls sharply from near to far, or vice versa. This usually involves measuring distances with a tape measure and having a separate person, the focus puller, to control the focus mechanism on the camera. This shot can be dramatic but is best avoided for sketches.

The main aim for TV sketches is to avoid complicated, time-consuming and therefore more expensive shots. Watch television programmes and note which shots have been used. Think about why they have been used and the effects they have achieved.

Try to visualize how a sketch is going to be recorded and be as imaginative as you can, but don't let fancy camerawork take over from the humour of a sketch. Anything which can be done in one continuous take without using different angles or cutaways will be looked upon more favourably by producers.

# Production considerations

## Continuity

Any sketch which calls for someone to smoke a cigarette or eat a meal may cause problems when shots from different takes are later edited together. Similarly, if anything has to be blown up, smashed or otherwise destroyed it will be difficult, if not impossible, to set the scene up for a second take.

There is a lot of technical wizardry which has made many things easier and quicker today, but these still do take extra time and resources. Let your watchwords be, 'Keep things simple'.

## Special effects

Chromakey or Colour Separation Overlay (CSO) involves filming against a blue background onto which film of something else is projected, so you could have the illusion of someone being in a lion's cage or skiing down a volcano when in reality they are safe in the studio. Weather presentations are produced in this way, which is why you never see the shadow of the presenter on the weather map.

Any special effect or illusion takes extra production and/or editing time, even if it is possible and the facilities and resources are available. Again, 'Keep things simple'.

## Studio sets

When using sets not specified in a writer's brief keep them simple and standard – house rooms, restaurant, office, for example. Castle interiors, space ships and distressed – dirty or damaged – sets are not so easy to build and will cost more. Keep the number of sets to a minimum: for a sketch limit it to one set.

Stairs are expensive to build and as studios don't have ceilings, any upward or high shots will almost invariably get lighting rigs in the frame. In the other direction, any sketch requiring a descent through a trapdoor or cellar steps will mean building the floor level up so there is something to descend from.

## Locations

The budget for a show will determine whether there is to be any filming on location (aka exteriors) as this is more expensive – there are extra costs of transportation, hotels if the location is not near the studio, insurance and catering. There have been sketch shows produced using exteriors in the grounds of studios, so this is one way around the problem.

Location filming can be quite precarious as the environment is not so controllable as in a studio. Factors such as the available light, the weather, unwanted (ambient) noise of traffic, aircraft, ice-cream chimes and members of the public may all affect filming schedules. Sketches which rely for their humour on sunshine or rain are not a good thing.

A writer's brief should specify if there is to be any exterior filming and unless you know particular locations are to be used, it is best to use general locations such as a street, a garden, a car park, which can be easily found anywhere.

Avoid having a sketch which involves night shooting as this requires overtime payments and extra equipment, and is therefore more expensive.

Dialogue should be kept to a minimum for exterior shooting and avoid having characters speaking as they move, as it is difficult to control sound levels.

## Costume

Modern day clothing is cheaper and more easily obtainable than period costume. There is usually no problem with using character costumes such as that of a biker, waiter, or in using uniforms, but it is sensible to bracket them if they are not on the writer's brief. Elaborate hair and make-up requirements should also be avoided.

## Props

Only specify essential props and avoid elaborate or expensive props – an ancient gramophone, Rolls Royce car or army tank may all be difficult to find.

## Cast

Keep the cast to a minimum and avoid the use of non-speaking extras. Also, keep in mind the skills you are asking of an actor. A stunt artist, accomplished musician or gymnast to double for an actor will cost extra money.

Animals, children and babies are more difficult to work with, and all have to be paid in the same way as actors do.

## Studio audience

Scripts for shows to be recorded with a studio audience will need to be written slightly differently. Time has to be allowed for audience laughter, but not in the way a comedian would stand and wait for the laughter to subside before continuing.

Don't give important information directly after a punchline, as it will be drowned by laughter, but do have a few inconsequential words of dialogue or action after the punchline so that if there is no laugh, it will not cause a gap. As with radio, a smile cannot be heard so make sure there are plenty of laugh out loud funnies in a script.

# Other considerations

## Star-led shows

If a sketch show is star-led you will need to study not only the show but the performer. Ask: What is he or she good at – impressions, physical comedy, singing, facial expressions, regional and foreign accents? Always write to a star's strengths, never his or her weaknesses.

Usually the star(s) will play the main part in a sketch, so write with this in mind. If the stars are a duo, it is generally best not to specify who should play which part, as they may be predisposed to argue over who gets the best role. In your script denote each piece of dialogue as 1st Person or 2nd Person.

For a duo, ask how do they work together? Is one person straight and the other funny, or do they both have strong comedy personas? Is there a stage rivalry between them or do they complement each other?

Think of how they relate to one another. The relationship may change as they take on different sketch characters but maintain a unity of relationship when they are playing themselves.

## All shows

Sketch shows will always want that which is new – new ideas, new formats and new characters. Use all the idea generating devices mentioned in Chapter 3. It is better to take old ideas and give them a twist rather than imitate. TV advertisements often use innovative and imaginative techniques, so use these as a source of inspiration.

When writing for an an existing show you need to make sure your sketches are tailored towards that show. Ask, does it use silliness, whimsy, slapstick, surrealism, exaggerations, parodies? Are the sketches mostly character based? Are one-liners used? Does it have a political edge, is it saucy, how politically correct is it? Is it contemporary, or does it have a touch of nostalgia? What kind of audience is it aiming to attract – family, young, wide ranging? Ask can you really see these performers and no others in this sketch.

## ⇒ To market

### Submitting material

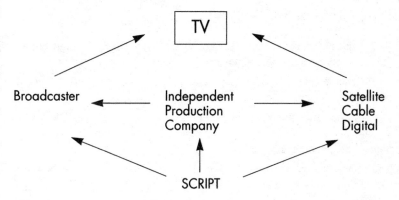

**Figure 8.1    Script routes into TV**

In Figure 8.1 you will see there are three main routes for the submission of scripts – to broadcasters, independent production companies and cable/satellite/digital channels. There are presently few opportunities with the latter channels and independent production companies are not able to broadcast their own programmes. Contact information for TV and independent production companies is given in the appendices at the end of this book.

With the number of broadcast channels increasing rapidly there are theoretically more outlets for your work, but on the other hand, budgets are becoming more fragmented. The trend does seem to be towards low budget programming which maintains high production values – it does not look cheap and nasty – and which will gain viewers.

Different TV companies may have slight variations in script layout when they go into production but it is acceptable to submit scripts in a standard format as follows:

Standard presentation, as described in Chapter 3, should be used with the exception that for a TV script everything is lined up half way across the page. The blank left side is used for camera directions, which you do not have to concern yourself with.

For sitcoms and other scripts with multiple scenes, begin each scene with an underlined scene heading denoting:

- the scene number
- whether it is to be filmed at an exterior location (EXT) or a studio or interior location (INT)
- where the scene is to be set
- the time of filming, for example, day, night, early morning or a specific time of day or night if this is particulalry relevant.

Begin each scene on a new page and use upper case letters for scene headings and speakers' names. Underline the latter.

For sketches and quickies which would generally only have one scene, you do not need to use a scene heading. Have a sketch title and your contact details on every page.

The main requirement is that there should be clear distinction between instructions and dialogue.

See Figures 8.2 and 8.3 for further reference.

---

**EXERCISES**

1 Make transcripts (or obtain printed copies) of several television sketches. Highlight where you think the laughs are. Think about how the set-ups and punchlines have been achieved. Be objective.

2 Write five sketches for television which are based in a restaurant.

3 Write up the sketch premises devised for television in Chapter 6 (see page 54).

# Layout

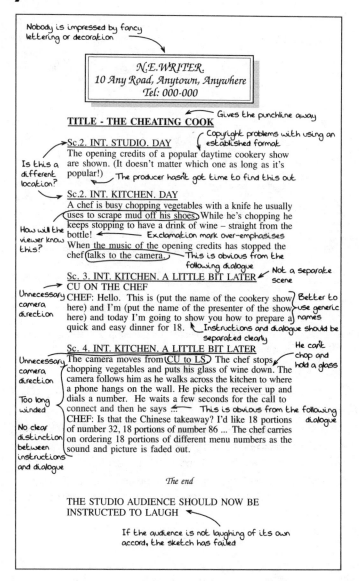

The annotations on the figure read:

Nobody is impressed by fancy lettering or decoration

*N.E.WRITER.*
*10 Any Road, Anytown, Anywhere*
*Tel: 000-000*

**TITLE - THE CHEATING COOK** ← Gives the punchline away

Sc.2. INT. STUDIO. DAY ← Copyright problems with using an established format

The opening credits of a popular daytime cookery show are shown. (It doesn't matter which one as long as it's

Is this a different location?

popular!) ← The producer hasn't got time to find this out

Sc.2. INT. KITCHEN. DAY

A chef is busy chopping vegetables with a knife he usually uses to scrape mud off his shoes. While he's chopping he keeps stopping to have a drink of wine – straight from the

How will the viewer know this?

bottle! ← Exclamation mark over-emphasises

When the music of the opening credits has stopped the chef talks to the camera. ← This is obvious from the following dialogue

Sc. 3. INT. KITCHEN. A LITTLE BIT LATER ← Not a separate scene
CU ON THE CHEF

Unnecessary camera direction

CHEF: Hello. This is (put the name of the cookery show here) and I'm (put the name of the presenter of the show here) and today I'm going to show you how to prepare a quick and easy dinner for 18. ← Instructions and dialogue should be separated clearly

Better to use generic names

Sc. 4. INT. KITCHEN. A LITTLE BIT LATER

Unnecessary camera direction

The camera moves from CU to LS. The chef stops chopping vegetables and puts his glass of wine down. The camera follows him as he walks across the kitchen to where a phone hangs on the wall. He picks the receiver up and

He can't chop and hold a glass

Too long winded

dials a number. He waits a few seconds for the call to connect and then he says ... ← This is obvious from the following dialogue

No clear distinction between instructions and dialogue

CHEF: Is that the Chinese takeaway? I'd like 18 portions of number 32, 18 portions of number 86 ... The chef carries on ordering 18 portions of different menu numbers as the sound and picture is faded out.

*The end*

THE STUDIO AUDIENCE SHOULD NOW BE INSTRUCTED TO LAUGH ← If the audience is not laughing of its own accord, the sketch has failed

**Figure 8.2    How not to write a TV script**

1                                    N.E Writer
                                     Any Road
                                     Anytown
                                     Tel: 000-000



QUICK AND EASY DINNER


A GENERIC TV COOK SHOW STUDIO SET


<u>PRESENTER</u>: And now we go over to Eva,

who is going to show us how to prepare

a quick and easy dinner for 18 people.


WE SEE <u>EVA</u> IS USING A PHONE


<u>EVA</u>: ... is that the Chinese takeaway?

I'd like 18 portions of number 50, 18

portions of number 32 ...


FADE OUT


**Figure 8.3      TV sketch layout**

# 9 | SITUATION COMEDY – 1

Situation comedy (aka sitcom, narrative comedy) is popular with programmers because of its relatively lower production costs and potential to keep viewers tuning in on a regular basis. Sometimes a rather maligned genre, writing a sitcom is nevertheless a very precise discipline which is not as easy to write as it looks, and should not be approached with a cynical attitude.

> Someone has to put a lot of sweat and craft into any sitcom and if you write with disrespect for the genre and craft, it just won't work.
>
> Sue Teddern, writer with *Birds of a Feather*

## What is a sitcom?

The definitions of what a sitcom is are blurring slightly today as programmers search for new and original variations. This chapter will look at the traditional sitcom format which you should think of as the basic model, and which you might later like to decorate as you please. Diverging from or developing the basic model is to be encouraged, as it is only in this way that imaginative and innovative sitcoms can be developed.

The traditional format has:

- humour which arises from the characters and situations they get themselves into, not a string of one-liners.
- self-contained episodes. While there may be story threads running through a series, each episode will have a story which is rounded off by the end of the episode.
- a 30-minutes broadcast slot.
- a regular cast consisting of a small number of characters.
- a small number of regular sets or locations.
- dramatic structure and narrative impetus.
- a recording with a studio audience.

# Special features of the sitcom

Sitcoms have a unique unity of both character and situation which is
maintained no matter how many episodes or series the sitcom runs to. This
serves to draw an audience into the world of that sitcom and its characters
and creates anticipation for the particular comic slant of that sitcom. How
is this unity achieved?

## Characters do not develop

Unlike drama where characters develop, sitcom characters are never
permanently affected by events and do not learn from their mistakes, or
change their lifestyle.

This is not to say you cannot be creative within that constraint. Writer Jim
Hitchmough moved the characters of *Watching* forward 12 months for
each series and John Sullivan gave Del Boy of *Only Fools and Horses* a
wife and child in later episodes. In neither sitcom was the basic premise
changed, nor the personality of the characters changed. There were the
same contrasts and conflicts, and relationships with other characters.

## Unity of situation

The basic 'situation' of a sitcom and therefore the basic source of humour
remains constant, no matter how many episodes or series the sitcom runs
to. If the situation changes, there is a different source of humour, different
relationships between the characters, and a different sitcom.

This is in fact what happened with *The Golden Girls*. When one of the cast
of four older women sharing an apartment left the show, it was decided that
the remaining characters should take over an hotel. The environment was
changed, which allowed the relationships between the characters to
change, there were different character hierarchies, and a different sitcom –
*Golden Palace*.

## Maintaining the status quo

Although the characters in a sitcom may take part in various comic
happenings in each episode, the original characterization and situation is
always re-asserted by episode end. Stories are orbital, rather than linear.

It is in creating a sitcom which is innovative and imaginative, which can
generate an infinite number of stories, yet still maintain the unities, that
the great skill and imagination of the sitcom writer lies.

## Ground breakers

*Red Dwarf*, created and written by Rob Grant and Doug Naylor, is set on a space ship manned by a bizarre collection of characters – pernickety hologram, a servile robot butler, a vain humanized cat, a computer, a Liverpudlian captain with a liking for getting drunk and eating curry and chutney sandwiches.

This would seem to be too oddball and unrealistic to fit the sitcom genre, yet with the emphasis being on the very human interaction between a few regular characters and mostly only two sets, the unities of sitcom are still there.

Other examples of sitcoms which have broken new ground are *Drop the Dead Donkey* which adopted the novel approach of recording some of the programme just before broadcast so topical references could be inserted, and *The Simpsons* which uses animation to bring originality to the sitcom genre.

# Creating an original series

In the US it is usual for sitcoms to be written by a team of writers and there are very few opportunities for the ordinary writer to develop an original sitcom. In the UK the majority of sitcoms are devised and written by individual or pairs of writers. There is an endless search for new and original sitcoms for both radio and television. When creating an original series you should be aiming for a clearly focused idea (situation) which can be succinctly described in one sentence, and elaborated on in a one to two page synopsis. Above all you should be aiming for strong, memorable characters.

During the planning stage you will need to define the best sets and locations for the sitcom to work on a regular basis, and devise storylines for subsequent episodes. We will look at each of the components.

# The 'situation'

The basic premise (aka basic idea, the scenario) of a sitcom is essentially the situation. It is what your sitcom is about and the source from which all the humour will evolve.

Aim to be able to state what a sitcom is about in one sentence. If it takes more than this, your sitcom probably needs a clearer focus.

A one-sentence description (aka logline) is also a useful shortcut selling tool. If you have the opportunity to talk to someone with influence, or you speak to them on the phone and are asked what your sitcom is about, you can tell them very quickly what the scenario is, the main character(s) and their comic flaw and motivation, and the main source of humour. If we look at how some sitcoms are described we can see that each has a clear focus:

> *Last of the Summer Wine*   Three old school friends in a Yorkshire village find themselves elderly and unemployed, so spend their days enjoying life.

> *Steptoe and Son*   The love-hate relationship between a frustrated rag-and-bone man and his exasperating old father.

> *Halliwell's Teleguide*

In each case there is an inherent incongruity, a conflict which if treated dramatically rather than humorously would be quite serious. They are ideas about which we have preconceptions and an understanding of the situation. They are ideas which have relevance.

## High concept ideas

A high concept idea is one in which there are a finite number of stories. *Duty Free* had the premise of two couples on a two-week holiday in Spain. There are only so many thing which can happen in two weeks. Similarly, *Only When I Laugh* was a sitcom about a group of men in hospital. Logically, they would eventually recover.

Despite having a very narrow focus both sitcoms were successful and ran to several series. The basic premise did become strained, however and involved contrivances to maintain the original situation.

## Low concept ideas

A basic requirement of a successful sitcom is that it has 'legs', that is, the situation will be able to generate an unlimited supply of storylines.

Low concept ideas have a greater ability to do this as, essentially, they are about basic human interaction in simple situations – four women sharing an apartment (*Golden Girls*) the people who meet up in a bar (*Cheers*).

Low concept ideas are ideally suited to a team writing system as the focus can be quite wide. If as an individual with an original idea, however, you propose a wide focus idea, for example, a group of people sharing a flat, it is more difficult to grab a commissioner's attention with a log line. You will then need to impress with your writing.

Within the parameters of high and low concepts there are four broad bands of 'situation', which we will now look at.

## Situations of place

When we talk of a situation of place we are not talking about the locale for a sitcom. *Last of the Summer Wine* takes place in Yorkshire, England but it is the four ageing delinquents who are the source of humour, not Yorkshire. The sitcom could be set anywhere and still have the same premise.

In a sitcom context, place is somewhere that particular kinds of relationships between characters exist, and will exist nowhere else but in that place. Examples include *Waiting for God* which is a sitcom about the people who live in an old people's home, *Desmond's* a sitcom about the people who come into a West Indian barber's shop and M*A*S*H, which is set in a Mobile Army Surgical Hospital in the Korean War.

When devising a situation of place, the place should be:

- ■ unusual or interesting.
- ■ somewhere in which lots of different things can happen.
- ■ somewhere which generates interaction between characters.
- ■ one in which characters can realistically and logically have ties which keep them there. They should want or need to be in this place for social, domestic, employment or emotional reasons. There should be no contrivances to keep the characters in that place.

## Situations of relationship

Here, the relationship between usually two, but sometimes more, people provides the source of the humour and generates stories. Again the characters need to be tied to that relationship by reasons of friendship, family, marriage, love, employment or whatever.

The ties of emotional and family relationships are the strongest which can bind people together, while also giving the most opportunities for the conflicts which can be turned to comic advantage. It is no surprise therefore, that domestic and romantic sitcoms are so abundant.

Always look for a different angle in a relationship situation. The family tie of a father and son is not unusual, but if they share a house, the father is elderly and able to manipulate his middle-aged son emotionally, then you have a *Steptoe and Son* (shown as *Sandford and Son* in America).

Other relationship situations may have an incongruity or conflict. *The Cosby Show* has a father whose family can never quite leave the nest, while *Who's the Boss* has the relationship between a male housekepper and his female boss.

You will need to be clear about the focus of a relationship sitcom as all stories should always have that relationship at their core. *Roseanne,* for instance, is not a situation of relationship, but one of character. It is Roseanne who provides the humour within the setting, not the other way round. There are no stories which do not figure Roseanne prominently, or which don't have an effect on her. Compare this with *The Simpsons* in which each family member may have their own story in the context of the family relationship.

## Situations of character

A situation of character will centre on one character who has a distinctive trait which will generate humour.

The character may give his or her name to the title of the series – *Roseanne*, *Ally McBeal*, *Frasier* – or the title may reflect the dominant trait of the character, for example, *Keeping up Appearances* is centred on the socially pretentious Hyacinth Bucket, or it may reflect the status or occupation of the character as in *The New Statesman* which is centred on Allan B'Stard, the roguish, womanizing Member of Parliament.

## Ensemble situations (Gangshows)

An ensemble situation is based on a group of people. Friendship is the tie which binds the characters in *Friends* together, as it does in *Golden Girls*. The workplace is the tie which binds the characters together in *Taxi* and in *Hi de Hi,* a sitcom based in a 1950s holiday camp.

It is easy for the focus of an ensemble situation to become dissipated with so many characters vying for attention. To prevent this, each episode should be written with a storyline focusing on no more than one or two characters, with the other characters then playing supporting roles in that episode.

It can be seen that an ensemble situation has greater sustainability as each character and the various combinations of characters will generate a greater number of storylines.

---

**EXERCISES**

**1** Study the basic premises of several sitcoms currently being broadcast. Ask what is the situation and is it a high or low concept idea? Make a note of the recurring characters, the number of studio sets, the proportion of exterior locations and the number of scenes.

**2** Devise two basic premises for each type of situation, such as place, character, relationship, ensemble. Don't worry about them being good or bad at the moment, as we shall be evaluating them in the next chapter.

# 10 | SITUATION COMEDY – 2

## Evaluating an original concept

Once you have an idea for a sitcom premise you will need to evaluate it. Programme commissioners may have a broad idea of the kind of sitcom they are looking for, such as something aimed at a younger audience, or a vehicle for a particular star, but mostly they want you to surprise them with something fresh and original. What they are quite definite about is what they don't want. There are a few questions you will need to ask of any sitcom premise.

### Is it a strong enough idea?

The commissioning editor or reader who is first going to look at your script will have hundreds if not thousands of scripts waiting for attention. Of necessity, they have to find shortcuts. Having that clearly focused, one sentence log line mentioned in the previous section will ensure your script does not fall at the first hurdle.

At the next hurdle, a synopsis should show the idea to be strong, in that it has 'legs', there is lots of potential for comic incidents and comic conflict, it has human values which an audience can understand and relate to, and that the characters are 3-D, realistic and are strong enough to carry the idea. An idea will also need to show it is strong by being fresh and original.

### Is it original?

An original idea? That can't be too hard. The library must be full of them.

Stephen Fry, *The Liar*

There have been thousands of sitcoms made, so it is difficult to find something which has not been done before. You can, however, avoid an obvious duplication or cloning by being aware of current output, reading trade newspapers and magazines with news of sitcoms currently in production, and consulting books which catalogue sitcoms (see Appendices).

A successful programme means that network controllers won't touch anything similar for years.

BBC Light Entertainment Radio,<br>guidelines for writing situation comedy

If you find your idea has been done before, it does not necessarily need to be thrown away. Perhaps the idea could be approached from a different angle, or be given a modern approach? Ask, could the same idea be done in a different setting or be given different characters? Could the situation be given a stylistic difference?

Ask what variations and twists could be given to a theme. For instance, *Steptoe and Son* has generational conflict at its core, as does *Keeping Mum*. The differences are that *Steptoe and Son* is a father/son relationship, while *Keeping Mum* is a mother/son relationship, complicated by the mother having Alzheimer's disease.

Always look for variations on the core of an idea.

## Will it date?

If you have an idea for a sitcom based on a current concern ask, will it still be relevant next year, in five years, ten years? A sitcom which is too narrowly focused on today is a high concept idea which will quickly cease to have relevance.

A parallel question will be, 'is it already dated?' It is sometimes difficult for older writers to realize the world is moving on and that it is not just fashions that change. Attitudes, trends, social behaviour, domestic and work relationships, even vocabulary, are all constantly changing. Unless a sitcom is set in a different era, it should be about today's people in today's world.

## Is it realistic?

Any piece of writing, sitcom or otherwise, should be true to the world created for it. The work should be realistic for the kinds of things that happen there and realistic for the kinds of people who exist there and act in that way.

If situations are contrived, just to make a joke, if characters do things just because there is a good chance it will get laughs, the world of that sitcom is not realistic. Everything should be credible and logical for the world created in that sitcom.

# Devising sitcom characters

> Good writers know their characters intimately.
>
> Seamus Cassidy, former Snr Commissioning Editor
> (Comedy and Entertainment) Channel 4 Television

You can have the best idea in the world but a sitcom is nothing without characters.

Whether you are writing a film, comedy drama or novel, there are many ways to originate characters. You can start from somebody you know in real life, begin with a quality such as thriftiness or miserliness, confidence or timidity, or use the potted descriptions of character which accompany astrological star signs.

Some writers like to write a whole biography of their characters. Even if all the biography is not used, if later it becomes difficult to think of more storylines, going back to a facet of the character may generate further stories.

If nothing else, a biography is a useful tool for getting to know your characters and, more importantly, understanding them. You will need to know your characters better than anybody else you know, better than you even know yourself. A viewer will not understand why a character is acting as they are, unless you know this yourself when you write.

The main priority with all characters is that they are individualistic, consistent, and plausible. There are some sitcoms where characters are not as we would expect to meet them in every day life, for example, the humanoid cat, hologram and other characters in *Red Dwarf*. They do, however, have realistic human emotions and interaction.

When creating your characters, ask questions of them, such as what are their aims and ambitions? What motivates them? Do they have fears and inhibitions, what are their likes and dislikes, what can they do well and what do they do badly? Keep asking questions until you find the unique individual which lies inside them.

Characters should be shown through action and not expositionary devices. Look for situations and interactions with other characters which will show what kind of person they are. Putting a character in a situation, or with people new to that character, and seeing how they act or react, will allow you to show deeper aspects of their personality. How will the insipid man deal with the glamorous woman who becomes interested in him? What will steelmen do when they become unemployed?

The questions will always be answered by characters who make things happen, whether by design, accident or failure to do something else. Things do not just happen to characters, characters are integral to making them happen.

You do not always have to put a character into a life-changing situation to reveal their personality. The best, or the worst, in characters can be revealed when they are stressed, drunk, during arguments, when something has caught them off-guard, when they are more relaxed, and also when they are pushed to their limits.

An excellent way of revealing a character is to take them to a crossroads, or to give them a predicament in which they have to make a decision. In the film *Bean, The Ultimate Disaster Movie* the incompetent and accident prone Mr Bean cleans the Mona Lisa and, in keeping with his character, wipes half the picture away.

There are many things a person could do in this situation – confess, hide the picture, blame somebody else – Mr Bean does none of these. He paints in the missing pieces. It is an unexpected solution which no one would ever take, except someone as naïve as Mr Bean's character, who believes no one will ever notice the difference. The incident is also visually funny when we see Mr Bean is no Leonardo da Vinci.

Characters also need clear motivation. Unless they are an illogical and scatty person, when everything they do will follow that pattern, they will have a logical reason for everything they do, and that logic should be consistent with their character. If we find we are constantly asking, 'Why did they do that?' more thought needs to go into the logic of character and action.

Give them unique dialogue too. (See also Chapter 7, Radio – Dialogue.)

## Comedy characters

Comedy characters are slightly different from the characters you would include in a more serious work, so we will look now at some of the distinguishing features.

- *Dominant trait or quirk* Comedy characters will always have the identity tag of a dominant trait or quirk. Some crossword dictionaries and other reference sources have lists of character types which you may find useful as a starting point.

  If a character is no more than this trait or quirk, they could very easily become a one-dimensional and predictable stereotype. They need to have other aspects to their personality, but which are still consistent and logical for their dominant trait.

- *Slightly larger than life* Not to be confused with exaggeration, this means that the distinctive qualities of comedy characters are just that little bit more sharp.

- *Empathy and identification* Sitcom characters should have basic human qualities and feelings which we understand and can relate to.

- *Achilles heel* A comedy character's weak point may be internal – insecurity, lack of self esteem – or it may be external – another person with whom they are always in conflict, or the world itself.

- *Greater disposition to fail* Heroes and heroines who succeed and win through may be the stuff of adventure, but the little person trying to survive a hostile environment is much better for comedy.

- *Self deception* The incongruity of how a person sees themself, and how others see them, makes for comedy.

- *Often weaker* Weaker characters will always come up against things they can't deal with. To stop them taking the easiest options, there will always be something, or somebody, stopping them running away and pushing them to do the things they do not want to do. This tension makes for heroic, and conversely, comic struggles resulting in things always going wrong.

■ *Fish out of water* Watching someone flounder or struggle to make the best of a situation can make for great comedy and give the poignancy of the little person trying to survive. You do, however, need to have a good reason for them being out of water, and at least make the outcome always in doubt, or it will become predictable. This comes back again to your character being tied to the situation.

## Unlikeable/undesirable characters

> Any man who hates dogs and babies can't be all bad.
>
> Leo Rosten speaking of WC Fields

Creating unlikeable or undesirable characters can be dangerous ground and needs careful handling. The bigoted and prejudiced Alf Garnett of *From Death Us Do Part* (transposed in America to Archie Bunker of *All In The Family*) received a fair bit of criticism: his views, however, were never put across as being acceptable, and he always got his come uppance by the end of the episode.

Generally, an unlikeable quality in a character will be a source of humour. The whining and complaining of the curmudgeonly Victor Meldrew of *One Foot in the Grave* brings him into comic conflict with people and situations which always get the better of him. The character also has truth, in that he is the voice of all the irritations and annoyances we meet in everyday life.

If characters who are less endearing leave the viewer with a sense of satisfaction, the character has got everything they deserve, there is truth, and the emphasis is on comedy, then you will not go far wrong.

## Plausibility of character

> Felix? Playing around? Are you crazy? He wears a vest and galoshes.
>
> Neil Simon, *The Odd Couple*

Whenever a character does or says anything it should always be plausible for them to act in that way, and if they do act out of character, there should always be a good reason.

There should always be logic and consistency of characterization.

## Names

> It was an odious, alien, distasteful name, that just did not inspire
> confidence. It was not at all like such clean, crisp, honest,
> American names as Cathcart, Peckem and Dreedle.
>
> Joseph Heller in *Catch 22*

Names will always have certain connotations – a Mabel or a George
suggests an older person; a Tracy or Craig someone in their twenties or
thirties; a Jade or a Jordan would probably be a child, while a Sebastian or
a Felicity is unlikely to come from a working class Yorkshire background.

If you give a character a name which seems odd or unusual, it could be a
distraction as the audience would always be wondering, how did they get
a name like that?

On the other hand, an incongruous name could say something about a
character's parents – names like Bianca and Racquel suggest an influence
from the glamorous world of films and entertainment. Additionally, if a
name like this was given to someone whose social graces and personal
hygiene contrasted sharply with that glamour, it could be quite funny.

Also, avoid using similar sounding names such as Ben and Len, Susan and
Sandra, which may lead to confusion. Think as carefully about naming
your characters as you would naming your own child.

## The cast complement

Sitcoms have a regular cast of usually around two to six characters and
you will need to decide who are the best characters for this situation.

First you will need to decide **what** the characters are.

Each character should have a job or function within a sitcom. Some
characters will go with the territory, for example, if you have a sitcom set
in a restaurant you are going to choose your cast complement from a
manager or owner, waiters, kitchen staff and regular customers.

Next, decide **where** your characters are.

There should be a hierarchy of characters with each having their place in
it. There will be a hierarchy of major and minor characters and within that
hierarchy there should be a hierarchy of those who make the decisions,
initiate action and get the most laughs.

Then you need to decide **who** your characters are.

For employment related roles, the characters will need certain qualities for it to be logical for them to have that job. Interview your characters as you would any applicant for a job and if you cannot see anyone employing them, give them another reason for being there – they've inherited the business is a better reason than they need the money. Money is not enough reason for a person to stay in a job they are unsuited for and dislike. They would logically find another job eventually and would not, therefore, be tied to the situation.

In a situation of relationship it also needs to be logical for those people to be together.

Now you will need to develop the 'who' side of your characters so there are the greatest possibilities for interaction.

## The cast – a network of characters

Each character in a sitcom should be different from all the others. You should be able to put any two combinations of characters together and get good comic interaction from their different personalities. This also opens up opportunities for the greatest number of storylines.

Each character, and more especially the major characters, should have someone who brings out the worst in them, someone who brings out the best, someone they can bounce off, someone they are in sympathy with and someone they will always be in conflict with.

For major characters, there should also be someone who fills the role of a confidant, so we can see inside the character. For example, in Carla Lane's sitcom *Bread* which centred on a mother with several grown-up children, we never saw the mother as a person in her own right.

In later series a next door neighbour was introduced and in addition to being able to provide an additional source of storylines, she could act as a confidant and sounding board for the mother.

---

**EXERCISES**

**1** Select any current sitcom and write short biographies of the characters. Make a note of how they interact with the other characters.

**2** Evaluate the ideas you devised in the previous chapter and select the strongest for further development.

**3** Devise a cast of characters for that sitcom.

# 11 | SITUATION COMEDY – 3

Sitcoms use a small number of regular sets for specific reasons. Sets cost time and money to build and there are only so many which can be fitted into a studio, and still leave room for an audience.

When considering the sets for a sitcom we are aiming to find three to four studio sets and will be asking:

- where is the best place for this situation to happen?
- which sets will have the most potential as arenas of action and interaction?

Think about why you need particular sets. Each set should have a stronger reason for being there than that of just going with the territory.

## Arenas of action

If you are writing a sitcom for radio where physical sets and locations are irrelevant, it is still useful to think in terms of arenas of action and interaction. We will divide these into main, public and private arenas.

### Main arena

This will be an area to which all the characters have access, and where they can meet naturally and without having to explain why they are there. Here are the main arenas of some existing sitcoms:

- *Roseanne* – living room
- *Dad's Army* – meeting hall
- *Drop the Dead Donkey* – newsroom
- *Fawlty Towers* – hotel reception area

The majority of the action and interaction in a sitcom will take place in the main arena. Here, we can have different combinations of characters interacting, or see all the characters together. As the main arena is common and neutral ground, there may not always be a clearly defined hierarchy among the characters.

## Public arena

This is secondary to the main arena. All or the majority of characters will have access to the area and the hierarchies may be more evident, in that it will be a domain in which a particular character(s) feels more at home, or has more control and power. The kitchen is Roseanne's domain and in *Fawlty Towers* Sybil's domain is the office, Manuel's is the kitchen, while Basil Fawlty's is the dining room.

A public arena may only be there to give a variety of set – the kitchen in *Golden Girls* for example – or it may be there to bring in interaction with other characters, as is the pub in *Only Fools and Horses*. A public arena's main function, however, is to allow for a different kind of interaction between characters than that of the main domain. It should also be capable of being used to generate different storylines.

## Private arena

A private arena is the domain of individual characters who will have clearly defined 'ownership' of that domain, although a lesser number of other characters may also have access to the arena. It may be a manager's office or a character's bedroom, for example.

This arena will allow for a different kind of interaction again, and will be a place where we can show the qualities of a particular character in more detail.

If you have trouble deciding on your arenas, go back to your main character(s) and decide where best you can show the plus and minus aspects of their personality, their inner and outer qualities.

Once you have decided on your major arenas, you can add another arena which will again allow for a different kind of action and interaction, or to give more interest and variety, but only if really necessary.

## Exterior locations

There should be a minimal amount of exterior locations used, as it may take hours if not days to shoot a few minutes of film, with all the additional costs.

This is not to say you should never use them – they do give variety, and may even be obligatory. A sitcom set in a stately home or garage, involving a sales rep or a gardener, would seem contrived if there were no exterior scenes.

If exterior locations are logical, they should be used, but sparingly – a total of four to six minutes is sufficient. If exteriors are needed for added variety, choose locations which are easily available such as streets and parks rather than mountainside or seaside, unless your sitcom is set there.

We now need to bring the premise, characters and sets together and decide what is going to happen.

# Storylines

> A half-hour comedy in many ways needs to be as tightly plotted as a whodunnit, with red herrings, twists and revelations – a series of unlikelinesses which end up making some kind of sense, however bizarre.

> > Pete Atkin, former Chief Producer
> > BBC Radio Light Entertainment

The plot of any storyline in sitcom should always develop from the original premise.

A storyline does not need to be anything of life and death proportions, it may be something as simple as a misunderstanding. In the same way the actual situation of a sitcom should be summarizable in one sentence: storylines too, need to be well focused.

> Unless you can summarize your plot in one simple sentence, it is probably too complex.

> > Melvin Helitzer

If we look at some listings tags for sitcoms, you will see how this works:

> Victor and Margaret are trapped in the garden shed for three-and-a-half hours by a swarm of bees.

> > *One Foot in the Grave*

There is an incongruity here, and if we know the characters, we can see that Margaret is going to suffer more than is usual from Victor's grumpiness.

> An MP concerned with the spiralling costs of the NHS is admitted for treatment.

> > *Only When I Laugh*

We can relish the thought of the MP getting a taste of his own medicine in this hospital-based sitcom.

> Lisa gets the silent treatment when she enrols in an all-male military academy.
>
> *The Simpsons*

From what we have seen of Lisa, we know she is going to fight back.

> Plot is essential because it reveals the characters.
>
> Seamus Cassidy, former Snr Commissioning Editor,
> Comedy & Light Entertainment, Channel 4 TV

For any storyline the characters will be presented with a problem, which it is important they solve, and which will set in motion a train of complications, misunderstandings and so on, the comic repercussions of which will involve all the other characters. How the characters deal with the problem (or don't deal with it) will have direct relevance for the kind of person they are.

Having a subplot, one is sufficient for a 30-minute episode, will give more depth and content. It should be interwoven with the main plot and the stories should relate in some way.

## Step outline

Once you have decided on the basic storyline and subplot, you should then develop a step outline. This is a plan of each stage of the stories in the episode.

The two greatest questions in plotting are, what if …? and what happens next …? Everything should have cause and effect, will confuse or complicate until there is a final resolution, which will bring the biggest laugh of all, or a satisfying rounding off of the story.

## Logic

There should be a logical reason for everything that happens in a plot. Events should be consistent with how these characters would behave, and if it is not how they would behave, there is a reason for that too.

The actual events themselves should also be consistent with the world you have created for that sitcom.

## Aims of the pilot episode

A pilot episode is often a speculative first episode made to entice programme planners and schedulers into commissioning a series, or it may indeed be the first episode of a series. The script which you will initially be submitting for a news series should be considered as a pilot episode. Its aims should be to establish the following:

■ the nature of the situation
■ who the characters are
■ the relationships between the characters
■ where and when the sitcom is taking place.

## Exposition

Get on with the story … Don't waste your opening scene giving the listener lots of what you consider to be essential information about your characters and the setting. Let all that emerge through what they say and do.

Pete Atkin, Chief Producer, BBC Radio Light Entertainment,
in a sitcom-writing competition guidelines

Information on characters' background and plot information should emerge naturally on a need-to-know basis. Don't have characters sitting around explaining things, or talking about things they have probably talked about many times before, but are doing once more for the benefit of the viewer.

Show, don't tell.

'Showing' is not just a matter of using the visual: it is putting characters in situations in which you can show them in action. It doesn't need, for instance, to be said that Basil cares about keeping the hotel open in *Fawlty Towers*, you would only need to show him fawning over a supposed Hotel Inspector.

If a character has a drink problem, show them drunk rather than have someone tell us about it. If a character loves someone, have them buy red roses, send a Valentine, slap on perfume or aftershave, or go over the top in trying to please, or gain the attention of their object of desire.

If characters dislike or resent each other, show them arguing, plotting humiliation, or trying to get the better of each other.

There are several devices which can be used to create comic situations in sitcoms: let's have a look at some.

## Plants

Plants are often a way of gaining funnies, anticipatory or otherwise. They are seeds which will grow and then bloom towards the end of the episode, but not in the way you expected. For instance, if a chair is broken it will later have to collapse as someone sits on it.

For example, at the beginning of one episode of *Watching*, Malcolm was making an anti-burglar gadget which sounded an alarm when the object it was stuck to was moved. The viewer was reminded about the device unobtrusively at one or two points in the episode. The unexpected payoff was that, in an attempt to prevent Brenda sleeping with Malcolm when circumstances meant she had to stay over, Malcolm's mother stuck the device to the door of Brenda's bedroom.

## Mental scripts

A character may have a mental script of what they will do if a certain thing happens, or a person behaves in a particular way, so if events don't occur or people don't behave as expected, then that character will have to rewrite their mental script.

If, for instance, someone says 'no' when a 'yes' was expected, the character will then be forced to do, or say, something they would not have thought of, or did not want to do. This will then take the story off in another, unexpected direction and another stage of the storyline will develop.

## Structure

Once have your step outline this will roughly determine the scenes. There will be a new scene whenever there is a change of place or time, and you should aim for a maximum of around ten scenes for a 30-minute episode.

Write a short summary of each scene (a few sentences) asking what is the aim of this scene? How does it move the story forward? If the scene does not do any of these things, take it out.

The story should have a beginning, a middle and an end. There should also be a hook, something to encourage the viewer to watch the next part, just before the commercial break, if the sitcom is intended for a commercial station. You will need to time current programmes to find, to the minute,

how long different broadcaster's shows run to without commercial breaks
or opening and closing credits. This will then indicate how long your
script should be.

As sitcom stories are orbital rather than linear, the status quo of the
original situation should be returned to at the end of the episode.
Remember to avoid using additional sets and additional actors, even non-
speaking extras, who still have to be paid for.

## ⇨ To market

### The submission package

Unless a particular company advises differently, a submission package
should consist of:

- ■ a synopsis of the situation comedy.
- ■ character outlines of two to three lines for each character.
- ■ a list of the recurring sets and locations.
- ■ a 30-minute script.
- ■ further storylines for five to six episodes.
- ■ your CV showing writing credits and any relevant
  experience.

You will need to make sure your package is received by the right person,
so use market reference books to find broadcasters and production
companies which may be interested in reading scripts. Write (with SAE),
fax, or telephone to check the information and to find the name of the
person to whom the proposal package should be addressed.

### Synopsis

A 'synopsis' (aka treatment, outline) is a one-page description of the
sitcom and should show the focus of the situation clearly and give an
introduction to the characters. The source of humour in the situation
should be implicit.

Commissioners can tell a lot from a synopsis and if you fail to interest here
it may mean the script is never read, or may be read with a negative attitude.

A synopsis is a framework on which to hang a sitcom and should therefore
have all the right pegs. Write it before you start on the full script and check

it again when you have finished writing the script to see if you have kept
on track. It may need some rewriting if you have thought of better ideas
or characters, but be sure it is still a well focused, but not too narrowly
focused, situation.

Don't wander into irrelevant details and facts. Mention the things which
will generate humour and show what is different, original and unique in
your idea. This does not mean however, that you should state this
explicitly. Rather than saying, 'This sitcom is original because ...', 'You
will laugh at this because ...' or 'Although this sitcom is set in an hotel it
differs from Fawlty Towers in that it is set in Scotland ...', **show** the
originality of sitcom through your description of it .

Think of a synopsis as a selling document. If you were trying to sell a
vacuum cleaner you would not enthuse about where it was made, or what
it was made of. A prospective buyer would be more interested in what it
does, why it is better than other vacuum cleaners, and all the other reasons
why they should buy it, rather than being overwhelmed with patronizing
sales jargon. As with vacuum cleaners, the potential buyer of a sitcom will
just want the plain and simple facts.

## Further storylines

In addition to your script, devise storylines for at least another five episodes.
These should be around a half to one page each and should show clearly that
you can maintain the basic situation, that is that the idea has legs.

## To send a complete script or not?

There are no hard and fast rules as to whether you should send a complete
script for a sitcom episode, as different broadcasters and independent
production companies have different requirements. You should make
initial enquiries before submitting a script. Nevertheless, it is usually
standard practice for a complete script to be requested of writers whose
work is not known.

Even if not requested, a complete script is something which is never
wasted. You are not only putting forward an idea for a sitcom, you are also
showing your writing abilities. A 'calling card' script may lead to
producers making contact to discuss any other ideas you may have for
sitcoms, or it may give you an introduction into team writing.

# Team writing

For the American system of producing sitcoms, team writing with several writers working on the same scripts is normal practice. At the time of writing, UK sitcoms using teams are the exception, and tend to be an adaptation of the American system. Although all team writers contribute to the development of series story arcs and storylines, scripts are generally written by individual writers.

## Making an approach to a team-written sitcom

First you will need to find out who produces the sitcom, then contact them saying you would like to join the scriptwriting team, and ask how you should go about this. If you have any comedy writing experience or credits, mention them here.

You should then be able to gain information on whether a specimen script written for the programme is required, or if they would like to see an original piece of your own work. Original work will need to show you understand the genre and its restrictions, that you can tell a story, identify comic situations and develop them to their full potential, and then resolve the story.

It makes sense, if the show you want to write for is realistic, not to send a surreal or zany sitcom, and vice versa. It should be written in your own style but not in a style which is totally remote for the show you're aiming for.

# A final word

It is not easy to gain a commission for a sitcom, even though the demand for original ideas is great. There is an enormous financial investment required of any sitcom and if you are an unknown writer you may find it even harder to get in with a sitcom which is an untried format. Getting your name known in some other related way, such as a sketch writer, stand-up comedian or as a playwright for radio or theatre, may be the key which will open the door.

Keep your eyes and ears open for opportunities – trade publications, an odd line on TV, radio or in newspapers may give a hint that someone, somewhere may be looking for sitcom scripts and/or ideas, or may give a lead to a particular kind of script being sought. Networking with other comedy writers through writers' groups or joining a professional comedy writers' organization, may also gain you information.

---

**EXERCISES**

**1** Define the best arenas of action for sitcoms on the following topics:
- a zoo
- a DIY shop
- train drivers
- a newspaper office.

**2** Take the following emotions and devise a scenario to show them in action:
- greed
- insecurity
- courage
- arrogance
- jealousy.

**3** Taking the situation premise and characters developed from the previous chapter, devise several storyline premises.

# 12 | THEATRE

*The world is a stage, the stage is a world of entertainment.*
**Howard Dietz**, *That's Entertainment*

Not to be overlooked when it comes to comedy writing, theatre is not just for plays, humorous or otherwise, it is the place your comedy sketch writing skills can be put to good use in revue style shows and where you can have real fun writing that most popular form of theatre – pantomime.

## Advantages and limitations of theatre

### Advantages

Theatre offers enormous scope for the imagination. If an audience is asked to believe an actor is holding the earth in his or her hand they will willingly suspend their disbelief and go along with the idea. A writer needs to use this power responsibly, not cheat the audience, and not poke fun at them for believing the unbelievable.

If you want to get actively involved in the production of your work and try things out with actors and an audience, then theatre is a real hands-on learning experience.

A TV or radio script may gain a repeat broadcast for which you will be paid accordingly. A comedy play, pantomime or farce, on the other hand, can be shown simultaneously around the country and abroad, and carry on being shown in different theatres for many years, with each performance bringing royalty payments to the playwright.

### Limitations

When writing for the theatre you do need to be aware of the limitations of the performance space, the practicalities of scene and costume changes and to think about actors' entrances and exits. Maintaining the three unities of time, place and action will keep things simple.

As theatre is live performance, complicated slapstick and acrobatic routines, especially if they involve props, will need a lot of rehearsal and will always have the natural inclination to go wrong on the night. Again, keep things simple.

You will also need to remember that those at the back of the balcony won't be able to see the joke which relies on a facial expression or small prop for its punchline, unless exaggeration is used.

# The revue

Revue shares some of the history of music hall, vaudeville, and the satirical traditions of burlesque but the modern revue takes its format of unrelated sketches, songs and other humorous material from the Cambridge Footlights *Beyond the Fringe* shows.

A revue show may be written and performed by and for students or other groups as an end of year or Christmas entertainment, a show put together for holiday camp entertainment or a satirical revue show, written by a small number of regular writers, or open to unsolicited scripts.

Alternatively, a group of comedy writers and musicians may put their own show together for performance in a hired theatre or hall. Many pubs will also offer the use of a free function room, or a local amateur dramatic society may be interested in putting on a revue, either written wholly by yourself (a massive undertaking) or in collaboration with other writers and musicians.

The length of revue sketches varies: shorter sketches can be used for variety or to link other sketches. Anything longer than around five to ten minutes will begin to slow the pace of a show, unless there are lots of laughs, music and other variety material along the way.

Keep sketches simple and costume and props down to a minimum. Have a good strong comic premise to each sketch and utilize the strong assets of dialogue and characterization.

A revue show will look disjointed and jerky if it consists wholly of one sketch ends, actors go off, other actors come on, next sketch begins. Think about getting into and out of sketches in a smooth and natural way.

If you plan to get involved with your own revue show, think of the order and arrangement of sketches, songs and other material. Have a strong beginning, something memorable at the end of act one to bring the audience back after the interval, and a strong ending.

Balance longer and shorter sketches and use music, limericks, stand-up comedy, monologues and other variety material as links. When working out the order of material, keep in mind which actors are in which sketches, so they have enough time to prepare for their next sketch.

Songs may be parodies of existing songs or original songs. Remember that royalties will need to be paid on lyrics and music if they are from another source. Advice can be obtained from the Performing Rights Society.

## The sketch show

Not *exactly* revue, the sketch show has become a feature in recent years. It may owe much to comedy writers having an excess of sketches over the amount of television shows to take them, but is nevertheless an option for theatre or comedy venue performance.

You will need to check out the performance space beforehand, and if you require them, the sound and lighting facilities. Many comedy venues only have performance space for stand-up comedy and a fixed microphone. You may find, however, that you could extend some sketches in and among the audience. Keep props and costume changes to the minimum and be imaginative in how sketches can be performed.

## The pantomime

Almost always guaranteeing capacity audiences, pantomime is a fun-packed entertainment generally aimed at a family audience.

Fairy stories or nursery rhymes provide the basic plots for pantomimes but from there, aim for originality by adding variations, changing the setting or the era, to give something which is a little bit different.

Include audience participation games and quizzes together with the traditional 'He's behind you, Oh, no he isn't, Oh, yes, he is' scenarios. If you know the audience or area include local and topical jokes.

Pantomimes are a whole entertainment and always have the colour and variety of song and dance routines. Special effects are often used but it is best to write scenes which leave the way open for variations on visual representation, unless you know the special effects, lighting and sound facilities available.

The characters in pantomime are simplistic with one strong characteristic – good, bad, brave, cowardly or whatever. Characters who are inept, clumsy or exaggerated offer lots of comic potential.

Too many characters can be confusing, especially for younger children, so keep the main action centred on a core cast relevant to the story.

'Stock' panto characters include:

- principal boy, usually played by a woman
- principal girl
- a dame, usually played by a man
- usually some kind of parental figures, for example Baron Hardup in Cinderella, Alderman Fitzwarren in Dick Whittington or the Emperor in Aladdin
- an assortment of goodies and baddies, clowns, pantomime cats, cows and other animals
- a chorus.

When writing the panto, balance dialogue and action between the characters so a few don't have all the lines and action, and keep track of which characters are on stage, for how long, and what they are doing. Characters should not be standing around doing nothing, or worse, distracting the audience, unless this is being used as a comic backdrop to offset a lengthy expositionary speech.

As there will be a family audience you should avoid bad language and innuendo. Humour which appeals more to the older and adult members of the audience can be included, but there should also be enough variety and interest to keep the youngest members of the audience from being bored and causing disruption.

Most amateur dramatic societies perform a yearly pantomime and could be interested in a script. You would need to contact them early on in the year so they can arrange their programme. Contact your local Arts Board or council Arts Officer for information on local groups. Their addresses can be found in market reference books.

Pantomimes and plays are often published and information on publishers can again be found in market reference books.

# The comedy play

> In the theatre words have to prove themselves immediately, by solid laughter which unites an audience, or by that attentive silence when even the most bronchial listeners forget to cough.
>
> John Mortimer

It is possible to write a series of sketches linked by a common theme and call it a play but it is significant that when such as Neil Simon, Alan Ayckbourn, John Godber, Oscar Wilde and Noel Coward write comedy for the stage, they are called playwrights rather than comedy writers.

> This play is a comedy, and so, like all comedy, it should not be played for laughs. It should be played for the truth in the lines. The laughs will come.
>
> Sue Townsend, introduction to *Bazaar and Rummage*

Those comedy plays which have stood the test of time and regularly attract audiences have proper story structure – a beginning, middle and end, conflicts and complications, good characterization, and comedy which has an element of truth. Witty turns of phrase and one-liners are fine, but should relate to character and situation and not be merely abstract jokes. Dialogue may be witty, it must also be insightful.

As with any dramatic work the dialogue should be speakable and tongue twisters and words difficult to pronounce should be avoided.

Dialogue should also be natural, individual and have the quality of being easy to remember by actors. Having a logical train of thought connecting speeches will help, and as actors take their cues from particular lines and movements, it avoids confusion if no two speeches have similar endings.

# The farce

Many comedy plays have farcical elements but the farce itself is characterized by exaggeration, broad humour and complicated plot in which everything goes wrong, clothing is lost, people are caught in compromising situations and mistaken identity and misunderstandings set off chains of unlikely events. It is orchestrated chaos resulting from characters, their relationships and situations rather than slapstick.

Although slightly detached from real life, a farce should also have poignancy and pathos, insight into human vulnerabilities, and empathy with their situations.

## ⇒ **To market**

Script layout for theatre is shown in Figure 12.1

**(TITLE ON EVERY PAGE)**                                              (PAGE NO.)


JAKESY              Do you have to go?

SANDRA              Don't tell me you're going to miss me.

JAKESY              Of course I will!

                                    SANDRA OPENS THE FRIDGE

SANDRA              When you're hungry, you take one of these, and you
                    put it in the microwave.

JAKESY              I can feed myself, you know!

SANDRA              Yes, you do know how to manoeuvre food into your
                    mouth. Your mother did a good job.

                                    SANDRA PICKS UP HER COAT AND
                                    WEEKEND BAG.

JAKESY              No wait! (HE DOESN'T KNOW WHAT TO DO
                    NEXT) I'll ... I'll make a cup of coffee and we'll talk
                    about it. (HE SWITCHES A KETTLE ON)

**Figure 12.1   Theatre script layout**

## Theatres

Comedy plays may be submitted direct to theatres and you should first consult market reference books or theatre associations as not all theatres are interested in new work or comedies.

## Theatre companies

Many theatres accept productions only from touring theatre companies. You can find contact details for this kind of company from theatre and playwrights organizations and Arts Boards.

## Amateur dramatic or theatrical societies

'AmDram' societies, as they are sometimes called, will often stage several productions a year – a classic play, a comedy, a musical and a pantomime is a common programming. They tend to use published plays for which they pay a small royalty. You may be able to interest them in a script of your own, but unless you are fairly well known in the area, you would need to prove it is a certain crowd puller.

## Publication

There are several publishers of plays and, again, information is available in market reference books. Published plays are available for production by theatre companies, schools and other organizations, who pay a small royalty for the right to perform them. The playwright is also paid royalties for each production.

## Self production

It is relatively easy to produce your own play on the stage. Some money is needed to pay a deposit on the theatre, and to buy props and costumes and publicity material. It is not usual to make vast amounts of money with self-produced theatre works but if the play is successful you may find the takings will cover all costs and anything left over is usually split equally between everyone involved in the production.

Theatres usually arrange their programmes in 'seasons' so you would need to book a theatre well in advance of the previous season to get into their programme literature. They will usually ask to read the script first. You will need to find out if you can use the theatre's light and sound technicians, or if you need to supply your own.

When organizing a self production you will need to:

- find the actors. You can contact actors you know, those you have seen perform in other works, or you can advertise and audition.

- find a director. A director is useful in keeping a play together and motivating the actors and can be found in the same way as actors.

- find rehearsal space. This does not have to be elaborate and expensive – many plays are rehearsed at home – but there does need to be sufficient space to work actors' movements and entrances and exits.

- organize a full dress rehearsal which should iron out any last minute difficulties.

- arrange for a technical run through of lighting and sound in the place of performance, which should eliminate any problems which might occur on the night.

- take advantage of publicity and promotion. Make the most of free publicity in listing magazines and on local radio, cable TV, and so on.

---

**EXERCISES**

**1** Rewrite the radio and TV sketches from the exercises of Chapters 7 and 8 for the stage.

**2** Using a published comedy play:
  - summarize the plot in one to two pages
  - outline each of the characters in a few sentences.

**3** Write an outline for a stage comedy play/farce/pantomime of your own devising.

# 13 | STAND-UP COMEDY

When a comedian delivers a set (aka their act or comedy routine) in a relaxed, informal way, peppering it with seemingly ad-libbed remarks and improvisation, it is easy to feel their material is all of their own making. This may or may not be true.

> To make people laugh requires a considerable amount of serious preparation and forethought.
>
> Gyles Brandreth

In fact, there are wide variations in the sources of a comedian's material. It may be all self written, or some or all may be from other sources, such as writers or gag sheets.

If an audience shouldn't be told the same joke twice, then a comedian doing live gigs (aka shows or performances) does not need so much material, as he or she will be playing to different audiences around the country. The core of the set can remain the same, with new material being introduced, tried out, honed and perfected on a gradual basis.

Increased success, however, brings returns to the same audiences, interviews and reviews which may quote examples of jokes, which then means they cannot be used in a set, and so there is a greater need for new material, and therefore a greater need for writers. If the comedian progresses to television, with its audiences numbering millions, there is a definite need for a writer or writers.

> I did six minutes near the end of each programme and I used up the material I'd spent five years putting together.
>
> Ben Elton, on making *Saturday Live*

Before you approach any comedian with material, first find out whether they actually require it. You can contact comedians through their agents and there is more information on this at the end of the chapter.

# Research

In order to write successfully for stand-up comedians you will need to research not only the medium of stand-up and live performance, but also the style and set content of the particular comedian you intend to write for.

Begin by making your research as broad as possible. Watch comedians on television, hear them on radio, or see live performances in a variety of venues – pubs, clubs, cabaret, theatres, holiday camps, cruise ships, universities, in talent contests and comedy festivals and, of course, dedicated comedy clubs. Supplement this with video, audio and album recordings where these are available. Think about why some comedians seem to be more successful in making an audience laugh than others, and think about how this has been achieved.

It is best not to write notes or record a comedian's set at a live performance – it may be thought you are stealing their material, but you can make transcripts of any recorded material. Include any interjections or verbal mannerisms which are made. Transcripts will make it easier to analyse performances, and will also show how a comedian's set looks in the medium you will be working – written words.

It may in some cases be painful, but watch the good, the bad and the indifferent. Some comedians will make you laugh, others will not. What you should gain is an understanding of stand-up comedy as more than somebody getting on a stage and telling jokes. There is an art and a craft and enormous variety among both comedians and the material they use.

# Comic persona

Any material submitted to a comedian should be tailored to suit them, so we will need to look at their comic persona. This is the particular personality, or identity they assume when they are on stage.

You may like to draw up a research sheet, as in Figure 13.1. This can then be filed along with copies of articles, reviews and other information on the comedian. Put the date on all research material as comedians change and develop their act over time, and you will want any material you write for them to be up to date.

If you intend doing stand-up comedy yourself, you will need to determine your own comic persona.

| **Name of comedian:** | **Date:** |
|---|---|
| Style | |
| Attitude | |
| Mannerisms | |
| Catchphrase | |
| Material Topics | |
| Material Form | |
| Act Structure | |
| Strengths | |
| Weaknesses | |
| Other comments | |

## Figure 13.1 Comedian research sheet

> ... but then I have a stage personality, it's not one that's different, it's just one that's very much more exaggerated.
>
> Steven Grant

While some comedians may use a persona which is, or is close to, their real personality, others may use the persona of a devised character. A comedian whose set is a string of straightforward unrelated one-liners on any subject may not have a persona as such, while others will have a very finely drawn and well-developed persona which serves as a strong identity tag, and will determine which comedy material they use, and how they use it.

A persona and their point of view should be consistent otherwise there will be a credibility gap. It would seem odd for a skinny person to be talking about dieting, for instance, or a left-wing radical to suddenly become the epitome of suburbia.

# Components of a comic persona

## Style

This will be the most unique thing about a comedian and is the particular rhythm, manner of delivery and unique twists which they give to their material. This is how the styles of some comedians have been described:

- exuberant (Ruby Wax)
- surreal and whimsical (Eddie Izzard)
- deadpan ... the master of understatement (Jack Dee)
- free-flowing, philosophical routines (Dave Allen)
- ranting, raucous and extremely foul mouthed (Gerry Sadowitz)
- political without being sanctimonious or preachy (Mark Steel).

Identify what is unique about a comedian, look for the adverbs and adjectives which best describe the style. There is no substitute for doing your own research, but reviews and interviews with comedians will help with research, will tell you how others see them, and will provide confirmation of your own views.

A comedian's style will also be unique in the approach they have to their material, even when different forms of material are used in longer shows. Ken Dodd, for example, uses songs, topical gags, one-liners, off the wall comments and short anecdotes, but has unity in that there is always a quirky, surreal element in all the material.

## Attitude

> Good comedians don't simply tell jokes, they act them out with a very specific emotional attitude.
>
> Judy Carter

The attitude should be consistent with the persona. They will have a range of emotions about different topics but the depth of the emotions and how they are portrayed will be consistent with the dominant attitude which may be sarcastic, aggressive, fatalistic, neurotic, couldn't-care-less, and so on.

## Topics/subjects

Once you know a comedian's persona you will be able to determine what topics and subjects that personality would talk about. It can also become an identity tag – Jo Brand is associated with the topics of chocolate, cakes, food generally, and satirizing the stereotypical characteristics of men and women.

You can draw up a character biography of a persona in the same way you would for a situation comedy character. You could also 'hot seat' the persona. This is a system which actors use for getting to know the characters they are playing, and involves having questions fired, and the actor answering as the character.

This will allow you to explore the main interests and obsessions of the persona, their angle on particular topics and what they find worthy of conversation. It should help with finding new and original topics, and new angles on existing topics.

## Devised characters

Some comedians appear as a character complete with the appropriate clothing, props, and so on.

You will need to define the persona of any devised character in the same way as any other persona, and the character will usually have a sharply defined and dominant trait from which the humour evolves, for example:

- 'The housewife superstar' (Dame Edna Everidge, played by Barry Humphreys)
- 'Alan Parker, Urban Warrior' (played by Simon Munnery)

## Impressionists

Impressionists will play a range of characters in one set, sometimes using no more than a pair of glasses and an ability to mimic voices which may be:

- *regional, cultural and international accents*. When writing for these kinds of accents avoid using them stereotypically. Research any accent you are not sure of so there are the right rhythms, phraseology and colloquial expressions.
- *impressions of personalities*. You should determine the main characteristics of the personality, their mannerisms and unique way of talking – then use exaggeration. Remember that the aim is to be funny. Attacking the

personality through an impression may land a comedian with a defamation or slander suit.

## Double acts

Two comedians working as a double act may perform sketch type material, or do a stand-up act in which their interaction provides an additional source of humour. The pairing of a 'stooge' who always gives the feed line and is the butt of jokes, while a more dominant partner gets all the punchlines, is a bit dated. Double acts today tend both to have their own comic personas. Double acts of 'odd couples' offer the most possibilities.

Look to see how a duo interacts, how they bounce gags off each other, and how they relate to the audience. Are they playing to the audience, or to each other with the audience being merely onlookers?

If the double act is just two comedians telling separate gags with there being little interaction between them, there is really no reason for them to be a double act. If this is the case perhaps a writer should wait until they either go their separate ways, or begin to work as a cohesive duo.

Material written for double acts should draw on the humour of their comic interactions, and the individual personas within the pairing. Sketch type material and scenarios can be used, in addition to one-liners, anecdotal material and observations.

# Forms of material

The basic forms of material for stand-up are one-liners, observations, anecdotes, shaggy dog stories and other forms which involve songs, props, physical comedy including slapstick, magic, ventriloquism and other devices.

## One-liners

One-liners used for stand-up material should have an informal conversational tone and can be adapted, expanded and used in conjunction with observations and other material.

For political humour, whether for one-liners or other forms, you will need to read the newspapers, have a balanced point of view and know what you are talking about. You may be able to stockpile funnies which have a longer shelf life. (See also Chapter 5, One-liners.)

## Observations

Observations will highlight, pinpoint or comment on the absurdities and incongruities of life, its institutions and people. An observation may begin, 'Have you noticed how ...' or, 'Did you see that ...' Using the present tense and active verbs will give greater immediacy.

A basic joke structure is still required, and there should be the equivalent of a punchline, or a funny sounding phrase or comment, at frequent intervals.

> Did you know the biggest cause of crashes is people falling asleep at the wheel – but they don't have a campaign, 'Don't drink milky Horlicks and drive, it's a killer.'

> Hattie Hayridge

Observations are not told in isolation, they are part of a conversation which flows from one topic to another. In the above observation, Hattie Hayridge began with other observations on driving, and then continued on from the Horlicks joke to talk about sleep.

## Anecdotes

Stories about funny incidents, real or supposed, can be enhanced by the use of descriptive language, witty turns of phrase and visual imagery. It is better if the incident is personalized by the comedian saying it happened to them, or someone they know, rather than it happened to 'a man' or 'a woman'.

> A bloke I know has a very low threshold of boredom, but at last he got a job that really suited him – testing mattresses in a bed factory. He didn't stay, mind. Couldn't stand the way they kept waking him up for tea breaks.

> Quoted by Frank Muir and Simon Brett, in
> *The Second Frank Muir Goes Into*

## A shaggy dog story

Shaggy dog stories are fanciful, contrived and very short, structured stories which work their way towards a punchline, which may be a twisted cliché. You may like to work out the mishaps in a story which ends 'people in grass houses shouldn't stow thrones'.

## Other forms

- *Comic songs* may be original, or parodies on existing songs – be careful of copyright restrictions.

- *Props* may be anything from a pair of glasses to a whole box full of bits and bobs. Used imaginatively they provide a launch pad for one-liners, observations and anecdotes. Props which look funny or can be used in a funny way will work best.

- *Physical comedy* may need to be choreographed if it involves a lot of movement and activity or gymnastics. Exaggerated nervous energy can be integrated into material and made part and parcel of the set.

- *Magic* is a specialist skill, but in the context of comedy it is more likely that the tricks will go wrong, or be successful in an unexpected way – it may be a plastic rabbit which is pulled from the hat, a live chicken may appear in the form of an egg. Alternatively, comic banter may be used with straightforward tricks.

- *Ventriloquism* can involve all the different kinds of comedy material. The doll or puppet should have its own persona, and be considered as a partner in a double act.

# Mannerisms/catchphrases/props

These are all a comedian's trademark or identity tag, but only become so after repeated usage. Not all comedians have identity tags of this kind, but if they do look to see how you can use it to get extra jokes, or use it as an introduction to the set.

*Props* are a visual trademark – Ken Dodd has a tickling stick, Tommy Cooper had a fez, George Burns a cigar, Dame Edna Everidge has her outrageous glasses.

*Mannerisms* are another visual trademark – Lee Evans has a manic, nervous manner which leads to excessive sweating.

## Catchphrases

Once on stage the variety comic had the perfect device for cementing a matey relationship with the audience: the catchphrase.

Oliver Double

Tending not to be used so much today, a catchphrase can establish audience rapport as Oliver Double suggests. A catchphrase can also act as an identity tag, bringing a comedian to mind in much the same way as an advertising slogan brings the product to mind. It is therefore a useful device on promotional posters. Try to find new and original ways of using and developing catchphrases.

# Material and the audience

In order to entertain an audience a comedian needs two requirements:

1 Material which is not only good, but appropriate to that audience.
2 Performance skills.

It is not within the scope of this book to go into details of performance skills, the concern is only with the comedy writer's place in the laughter triangle, and how writers complement and support performance skills by supplying a range of material to suit different occasions, venues and audiences. (See also Chapter 2, The nature of comedy – The laughter triangle.)

## Set content

> If an idea is worth expressing, any way of expressing it is OK. But, be sure that you understand the group you are talking to or writing for.
>
> Barry Took

On the content of a comedian's set, religion and politics are always risky targets and while bad language and risqué material is acceptable to some people, to others it is not.

Some material will be insensitive in certain situations, for example, euthanasia funnies won't go down very well with an elderly audience, while many venues have a ban on sexist and racist material.

Appropriateness is not just about the use or non-use of controversial or insensitive material, however. It is also about including material which a particular audience can relate to – students and young people, for example, have their own cultures. Certain topics will have more relevance to them than to an audience composed mostly of elderly people, and vice versa.

Many comedians when appearing live, like to establish a rapport with the audience and make it look as though a set has been personalized by including local references – something the country, area or venue is famous for, its unique qualities, unusual or interesting features, notable personalities and so on.

This information can be found by reading about a place, talking to people who have been there, using travel guides (make sure they are up to date), contacting tourist offices, or speaking to the venue manager.

Unless a comedian originates from the area, all material should be written from the point of view of an outsider. The area and/or its people should also not be made the butt of any jokes – it may be taken personally.

Assessing what kind of audience is in – whether it is rowdy, subdued, sophisticated, in holiday mood or whatever – is not a precise science, but how an audience is arranged can make a difference. A theatre audience in formal rows has to be handled differently from a pub or club audience arranged café style, or a cabaret audience who may be eating and drinking.

In a theatre there are no distractions, and heckling is only easy if you are sat on the front row and/or can shout loud enough. An audience is therefore more likely to sit and listen, and longer anecdotes and observations can be used. It is somewhat harder to make a theatre audience laugh however, as there is not such an intimate, shared atmosphere. (See also Chapter 2, The nature of comedy – Social context.)

In a venue where there are the distractions of people going to the bar or toilets, where people are drinking or eating, a comedian has to fight harder to gain the attentions of an audience. Anecdotes will work if there are laughs at frequent intervals but longer, more involved stories will not receive the level of attention they require.

When there is the least audience concentration and the greatest distractions, one-liners will work best. The space between set-up and punchline is shorter, so there is less chance of missing something relevant to understanding the joke, and if it is missed, there will be another one-liner along in a minute.

## Heckle busters

It's a bit like drowning – if you're in danger your mind works astonishingly fast and you're constantly scanning for things to refer to, going through your material to see if there's anything appropriate, looking at the person to see if there's anything you can use.

Alexei Sayle

There is no doubt that heckling is a fact of life in live comedy, the smaller and more informal the audience arrangement, the greater its frequency. On some occasions it achieves the status of a sport.

Some comedians have their own devices for dealing with heckling. Ben Elton, for instance, uses a rapid delivery which leaves no room for heckles, while others may use music or physical comedy to change the mood.

Whatever means of dealing with heckles is used, it is all about preparation, and the writer who can supply a stock of good heckle busters will be more than welcomed.

## Controlling the situation

Responses to heckling which could become a personal shouting match between comedian and heckler, which in turn will lead to more heckling or even violence, should be avoided.

Good heckle busters aim to get the audience on the side of the comedian, redirect and change the mood from that of heckler and comedian in battle, to that of dual participation in making a joke. A comedian has to be able to stay in control of the situation and still be funny.

> 10,000 sperm, and you had to be the one who got through.
>
> Jeff Green

In this line of Jeff Green's the tone implies the heckler is a pain, but ironically, the heckler is also credited with being a biological winner. This duality makes it much more difficult for a heckler to respond negatively, and meanwhile the comedian has moved on to telling the next funny.

## Heckles as feed lines

Comedians will often repeat a heckle – not all the audience will have heard the heckle, and if it is not repeated, the suitably witty retort will be meaningless. It also gives a comedian time to think of that witty retort.

If heckle and witty retort are put together, we can see this parallels the structure of a one-liner. We would not, of course, be able to anticipate what every heckler is going to say, we can nevertheless anticipate variations on the most common heckles such as 'Get off', 'You're not funny' or 'I've heard it before,' and treat these as feed lines.

Brainstorm on everything connected with the situation and the people involved until you find something which can be used to create a funny line. Go off at a tangent to a related topic, or make use of the predicament itself.

## Insults and put downs

> Nightmare on Elm Street – the hairstyle. Freddie's back and this time he's got scissors and cutting gel.
>
> Lennie Henry

Insults and put downs are standard heckle busters and these can be prepared on a range of generic topics such as dress sense, hair, facial features and vocal capacity.

## Bombing/dying

> Just because the last act was bad, there's no need to take it out on me.
>
> Steve Allen

The reverse of heckling is the absence of any audience response. A performance device might be to go straight on to the next joke so there is no embarrassing silence, while a stock of funnies can be prepared ready for such a situation.

## Other prepared lines

Lines can also be prepared for events such as someone arriving late or getting up to go to the bar or toilet, equipment failure or forgetting a punchline.

# Set structure

> I do a set list because I think my subconscious will take it in ... if I have a photographic memory of writing something down on the set list, then happily it'll come back.
>
> Jason Byrne

Some comedians may only need a list of basic ideas or props before a performance and will then run through their thoughts and opinions on stage.

Planning the structure of a set, however, will not only ensure there is flow and momentum, it will also help with memorizing a set, as we will see later.

When working out the structure and order of gags in a set you may find it useful to write all the gags on separate sheets of paper or card, which you will then be able to sort and arrange. If using paper, tuck the edges under a ruler so they do not blow away if someone opens the door.

Once you have decided on the order, a key word or words can be transferred to one sheet of paper for easy reference.

A set should have a beginning, a middle and an end, each with a distinct function and aim, and requiring different kinds of material. We will look at each of these sections in turn.

## Openers

> Your opening is the most important part of your act. Within ten
> seconds an audience will decide whether or not they like you.
>
> Judy Carter

Some comedians are so famous they need no introduction, but for others a succinct, appropriately witty line or phrase with which a compère can introduce them, will create a positive atmosphere before a comedian even sets foot on stage.

When a comedian goes on stage, in addition to trying to calm their nerves, he or she is aiming to establish a rapport with the audience.

If you think of comedian and audience as being two people meeting for the first time then this will help with deciding on opening material. It should not be clichéd or use empty words just to get into the act, and any controversial material should be saved until an audience knows the comedian a little better.

A set should be opened with the strongest material which has been tried and tested. This gives greater feelings of confidence, will lessen nerves, and there is more certainty of getting laughs.

We looked earlier at relating material to an audience, and any material which has been specially prepared for that locality and audience will act like the hand of friendship when used near the beginning of a set.

Many comedians will begin their set by making jokes about something distinct or obvious about themselves, such as their size, name, a disability they have and so on. This is a basic way of a comedian telling an audience something about who they are and their tone and style of comedy. More importantly, it gives their attitude towards themselves, which will be a cue to how an audience should feel about them.

# Middles

The middle of a set will contain the main bulk of funnies. It should be flexible enough to allow for a comedian to respond to the audience or environment with ad libs, prepared or otherwise, and to be returned to without it seeming to have been interrupted.

### Middles – compartments of funnies

To do this we need to think of a set as a series of compartments which can be left by any of several doors. Thinking in terms of compartments will also help with memorizing both the funnies, and their place in the set.

### Middles – mind webbing

An example of mind webbing is a sequence about London tube trains which was used by comedian Alan Davies and which shows the creation of a flexible structure for a compartment of funnies. (See also Chapter 3, Beginning comedy writing – Mind webbing.)

Having established the theme of travelling by tube, Alan Davies went on to talk about inside the carriage, and mind webbed to tell funnies about what was in there – the people, the seats, the heating and the doors. Having got to the doors, he then focused attention outside the carriage, and had funnies about the platform and then the station itself. Helping with the mind webbing was the logical progression of a journey around the carriage, getting off the train and moving through the station.

If any individual funny did happen to escape Alan Davies, it would not have mattered, there were others focused on the same locality. Also, if he had to interrupt the sequence for any reason, for example to ad lib or deal with hecklers, there were many points that could be returned to. If necessary, it would be quite easy to abandon the sequence altogether and go straight to another compartment of funnies.

### Middles – links

The funnies based on the inside of Alan Davies's train carriage were linked by their locality, but we also have to think of linking different themes or topics. In the sequence mentioned above, Alan Davies progressed to talk on the theme of cycling and bikes, which is linked with trains by the theme of travel. If we remember where we left the sequence, at the train station, you will see that moving outside to talk about roads, and what may be on them, is a natural progression in the journey.

Not all compartments of jokes will lend themselves to linking this well, and you may have to link similar or related topics by writing a few extra lines. The main thing is to ensure there is a logical flow between compartments.

### Middles – rule of three

Using the rule of three in the body of a funny can create a compartment of jokes, and if the structural ascendancy (or descendancy) of the rule of three is remembered, then the order of the three is easier to remember.

The following example grew from the idea that although some say comedy is beneficial, comedians should not exaggerate their own importance ...

> No one on his deathbed has actually said, 'I think the end is near, send for a comedian.' No airline pilot has ever told his passengers, 'Ladies and gentlemen, I'm sorry to tell you, but the engines are out, we're about to crash into the ocean, but thank God, we have a comedian on board.' I don't think you'll ever hear a Government Minister on *Question Time* saying, 'The Middle East crisis deadlock, it must be tolerated no longer – send in the clowns.'
>
> Bob Monkhouse

## Endings

Any comedian will want an audience to go away with positive if not fond memories of them, so the end of a set should be both strong and memorable. It may not always get the biggest laughs: some comedians like to end with a thanks and goodbye to the audience, a homespun proverb, or a song.

## ⇒ To market

As comedians do not always advertise the fact they use writers, how do you find out who might be interested in your material?

## Contacting performers

Comedians can be approached by either writing or faxing their agent. Contact information can be gained from 'Showcall' or 'Artistes and their Agents', details of which are in the appendices.

When making an approach, say you would like to write material for consideration by the particular comedian. Mention any comedy writing credits or other comedians you may have written for, and include a sample one to two pages of suitable material. This should then elicit whether that comedian is in the market for material or not.

Alternatively, find out where that comedian is appearing – look in listings magazines, newspapers; use Teletext, Internet sites, publicity brochures and leaflets – and send a letter and a sample of suitable material to one of the venues they will be appearing at, to arrive for the day/days they will be appearing.

If they are appearing locally, most performers hold an autograph signing and meet-the-fans session after a show, so you may be able to introduce yourself here. Have some suitable material ready to show, ask if they would be interested in you writing some material for them, and if this is the kind of thing which they would be looking for.

While it is nice to be able to write for top comedians, it is more difficult to do this: they often have their own writers and there is more competition. Therefore, it is worthwhile considering writing for a less well-known comedian, or an unknown comedian. You may be able to have more input into their act as a whole, you can build up a worthwhile working relationship, and spotting who is going to make a top comedian when they are in the early stages of their career could have the bonus that, as their career progresses, you go with them.

Look for a comedian whom you like. Then look to see whether they are relaxed and confident, have a strong stage presence, good timing, good rapport with the audience and the essential requirement which says a writer is needed – lousy material.

## What can you expect to be paid?

Material written specifically for a comedian is usually bought outright with payment rates for one-liners, longer jokes or whole routines being negotiated between the writer and the performer. Some comedians may pull cash out of their pocket, or write a more substantial cheque there and then. Others may want to try out the material first.

Some writers use the payments which would be received for one-liners at radio broadcast rates as a yardstick, while some comedians have very different ideas about what they want to pay. It is a very informal system, and there are no guidelines or union agreements.

You will need to play it by ear, and negotiate the best terms which you are both happy with. Keep in mind whether your material is earning a comedian money in paid bookings or, if early on in their career, they are doing only open mic spots (a session during a comedy club evening when the microphone is open to anybody who wants to do a short, often unpaid, spot), and therefore not earning any money.

---

**EXERCISES**

1 Write a short set of two to three minutes using anecdotes on the place where you live or work.

2 Using the one-liners you wrote for the exercises in Chapter 5, work them up into a structured set.

3 Write five heckle busters targeting a heckler who is drunk.

# 14 | CARTOON AND COMIC STRIP, GREETINGS CARDS

Even if your artistic ability is nil, you can write for cartoons and comic strip, where comedic ideas, funny stories and sharp captions are just as important as the visuals. You will also be able to use the same techniques to write for the greetings card market, and while writing something for an artist to bring to life can be satisfying in itself, it can also help in developing the visual awareness needed when writing for TV and film.

## Some basic considerations

- ■ *Greater subtlety* Cartoon and comic strips are a visual medium but as a reader can turn back and re-read a story, there can be greater subtlety.
- ■ *No financial restrictions* Cartoon and comic strips have an advantage over other visual mediums in that there are no financial restrictions on cast, costume, props, sets or locations.
- ■ *Restrictions of space* There is a limit to the amount of information which can be put into a frame, and a finite number of frames in which to tell a comic strip story. Inner conflicts, abstractions and extensive exposition will need to be avoided as not only do they slow a story down, they take up too many frames. A story needs to be told clearly and concisely through a series of freeze-frame incidents which are visually interesting. Complicated plots, subplots and story depth may need to be limited.

## Writer/artist relationship

Writers with artistic abilities can of course do their own artwork, while less able writers could use collage, photographs or computer generated graphics to create their own visual images. While the majority of one frame cartoons are created by a single person, however, comic strips are generally a collaborative effort. The American comics' system, for instance, uses writers, letterers, inkers, colourists and artists, while the UK system generally uses writers and artists, with bigger organizations more likely to have a split between the two.

# The script

Ideas are communicated to an artist through the medium of a script. There should be standard presentation as mentioned in Chapter 3. Figures 14.1 and 14.2 show script layout and how this relates to the eventual pictures.

A script should not dictate or stifle an artist's creativity but giving clear concise, unambiguous instruction will ensure an artist knows exactly what you want.

TV script terms for the size of shot – CU, MS, LS – are used to describe the pictures and, similarly, FX is used for sound effects such as 'Smash!' or 'Kerpow!' The artist will then know to represent the sound effect graphically. (See also Chapter 8, Television – Camera terms.)

In any script, words and pictures should complement each other and although you will see many cartoons and comic strips of the 'talking heads' variety, the better ones make imaginative use of words and pictures. As this is a visual medium, words should not be used if a picture could do the same job.

## Frames

A frame is a single picture and in a script, each should be numbered and have a description of the picture it is to contain.

Frame content should be kept simple and extensive detail of background, objects, clothing and so on should not be given, unless it is of particular relevance to the story. Artists will not take too kindly to a script requiring the drawing of a 100-piece orchestra or a crowd of 2000 people, and again the advice is, keep things simple.

Differentiate between frame foreground and background in your script. Backgrounds should not be too elaborate, or detract from the foreground.

N.E. Writer
Any Road
Anytown
Tel: 000-000

GRAN – SCRIPT 1

1. CAPTION    Second childhoods are a marvellous invention …

   PICTURE    A children's playground. Gran is riding on a roundabout
              with Mandy while Jason pushes it around. Indicate the
              roundabout is going fast.

   MANDY      Wheee!

   JASON      Is this fast enough, Gran?

2. CAPTION    Except for one thing …

   PICTURE    A piece of wasteground. Mandy and Jason are playing
              happily among the muck in the background. Gran is
              busy digging up daffodil bulbs.

   GRAN       I'll be able to plant these in our garden!

3. CAPTION    … Parents always spoiling the fun!

   PICTURE    At home. Carol is telling Gran off. Jason, Mandy and
              Gran are very dirty, and looking guilty.

   CAROL      You got them dirty, Mother, you bath them!

                                                        ends

**Figure 14.1  Example of cartoon script layout**

**Figure 14.2 The resulting cartoon strip**

## Captions

Captions should be used sparingly and only for necessary explanation, or for changes of time or place such as 'suddenly', 'later' or 'next door.'

Both captions and dialogue should be written in the order in which you want them to be read. The logical reading sequence is from left to right, and top to bottom. It is important to give clear instructions to an artist, as a punchline or plot revelation could be lost if dialogue or a caption is read in the wrong order.

## Dialogue

Dialogue should be natural, individual, readable and brief. There will not be room for more than 25 words in a frame: long conversations take many frames and should be avoided. (See also Chapter 7, Radio – Dialogue.)

## Speech bubbles

Speech bubbles (aka balloons) are not merely a device to contain the dialogue. Used creatively they can give a visual representation of mood, tone and emotion. A bubble with a jagged edge, for instance, can indicate fear, stress or terror, while a wavy edged bubble can represent a wobbly, scared voice.

Different kinds of bubbles can be used for different characters, either for identification or to show they are not really communicating, and overlapping bubbles can be used to show people are talking over each other.

## Think bubbles

Cartoon and comic strips have an advantage in that they can not only show what people are saying, they can also show what people are thinking. This can be used to show the irony of opposing or complementary thoughts and actions.

A think bubble is indicated in a script by writing (THINKS) at the beginning of the speech.

## Lettering

Lettering, too, can be used for visual interpretation of mood and atmosphere not only in dialogue, but also captions and sound effects.

Bold or upper case lettering can be used for emphasis, or when someone is shouting. Thin spidery lettering can indicate a weak person, or small lettering a person who is whispering.

# Forms of cartoon and comic strip

## Spot cartoons

Single frame spot cartoons are basically a visual one-liner. There are many spot cartoons around in which either the words or the pictures are not needed for the joke. The best, however, make use of both words and pictures.

It is unusual for spot cartoons to be created by a writer/artist collaboration but you may be able to interest an artist in one-liners which are suitable for cartoon interpretation. Many newspapers and magazines have regular slots for spot cartoons. Look to see if different cartoonists are used as this will then suggest they may be open to unsolicited submissions. Specialist and trade magazines may be particularly keen to see spot cartoons related to their particular subject.

All cartoons need to be drawn much larger than the size they are actually printed, so to reduce effectively, drawings must have simple, bold lines and lettering.

## The cartoon strip

A regular feature of many newspapers and magazines, the cartoon strip is a three to four frame self-contained story/funny about a recurring character or characters. As newspapers and magazines do not usually have their own artists you will need to collaborate with an artist and submit finished strips.

To find an artist with cartooning ability try contacting colleges which run art or cartoon courses, placing a newspaper or magazine advertisement, or contact a professional cartoonist's organization (see appendices).

If working with an artist to submit a complete package, ask if roughs can first be drawn. Any problems with the realization of the script, spelling, the arrangement of bubbles and captions and so on can then be discussed.

When devising a cartoon strip it is important for the idea to be sustainable over many years. Characterization is important as readers will want to know, love and laugh with these characters on a regular basis. Characters should be truthful, consistent and three-dimensional. Give them a recognizable viewpoint or philosophy which has the potential for unlimited funnies.

As with sitcoms, cartoon strip characters do not develop. If Garfield were to become a friendly cat who cared about spiders, dogs, exercise and healthy eating, the premise of the strip, and the personality of Garfield, would have changed and credibility would be lost.

The world of your strip needs to be one in which many things can happen to those characters: they do not have to be big or dramatic things, just ordinary everyday incidents, thoughts and consequences consistent with those characters in that place or situation. See how cartoon strips such as Garfield, Dilbert and Peanuts have stood the test of time with their unique perspectives on the ordinary and everyday.

When writing a cartoon strip have a synopsis of the basic premise of the strip, its style and tone, together with character outlines. This gives both commissioning editor and artist a general overview of the intentions of the idea.

The structure of the story in a cartoon strip is somewhat similar to that of a one-liner. The first frame will set the idea up, the second/third frames will run it along, and the final frame will round off with a punchline.

When submitting a cartoon strip you will need to prove you are able to meet the challenge of producing it on a regular basis. A basic submission package should consist of a synopsis and at least six finished strips. You should then have many other ideas ready. If you cannot find enough ideas, maybe that strip does not have sustainability.

Without much experience in producing cartoon strips, a daily paper is probably not the best place to submit your first strip. Your local newspaper, however, may be interested in something which has local relevance, or you may be able to interest a local or national magazine.

## The picture story

A picture story may be self-contained or a serial covering one or more pages of, for example, children's and youth comics or superhero comic books. You may be able to submit a script for an established story, or devise an original story.

When writing for an established publication, get hold of any writer's guidelines which may be available and study several copies of the publication too. Ask the following questions:

- Who is the average reader? What are their interests, ages, gender?
- What is the style and tone of the publication?
- Are there always the same number of frames to a page?
- How many pages do stories go over?
- Is there a variety of stories, or are they all of the same genre?
- Are both stories and serials used?
- Is the artwork black and white or colour, or are both used?

Some comics show an extremely creative use of frame shape, size and arrangement, often artist-originated, while others use a more regular arrangement with a standard number of frames per page. Aim to be as imaginative as you can within the format of the comic you are writing for.

### Picture strip – the script

You can write the picture story script as a narrative first, and then you will need to reduce the story to a series of plot points or incidents equal to the number of frames you have available. With space being limited, every frame has to earn its keep and if a frame does not move the story forward, reveal character or provide comedy, it should be taken out.

On the script itself, you will save a lot of explanatory detail for individual frames if at the beginning you give the general atmosphere in which you want the story told, such as menacing, whimsical, cute, gloomy or happy. The artist can then be left to do the visual representation of that atmosphere.

Frames are linked in much the same way as television shots and cutting at the right point is important. Avoid beginning the next scene or sequence of a story in the last frame of a page (orphan frame) and avoid ending a scene or sequence in the first frame of a page (widow frame).

Remember: pace is important. It takes around seven to eight seconds to read 35 words of dialogue, and around three seconds to look at a simple picture. Increased wordage and elaborate pictures will slow the pace down, while less wordage and simple pictures will speed it up. Silent frames with no words can be used to extend a moment of suspense or to give a pause before a punchline frame.

## Photostories

Photostory scripts are written in the same way as for picture strips. There are, however, greater restrictions on locations, costume and the number of characters.

# Greetings cards

There has been a rapid expansion of the humour ranges of many greetings card companies. It seems we all want to make someone smile.

Ideas alone are bought and the greetings card market can often be an extremely lucrative outlet for one-liners. A card will have the visual and/or verbal equivalent of a feed line on the front, and the equivalent of a punchline on the inside.

'Sendability' is an important aspect of any greetings card joke, so abstract jokes which are not saying anything are not the thing to write. More personalized jokes containing the words 'I', 'me' and 'you' are much better.

A browse through the racks of any card shop will give names of greetings card companies producing a humour range, or you can consult market reference books.

Some companies like ideas to be submitted on 4 × 3 cards, others will take paper submissions, while others do not have any preferred layout styles, so long as it is clear what goes where, and there is enough information for an artist to work on. If it is fairly obvious what the picture should be from the words, there is no need to give instructions to the artist. If you do have any particular ideas for the way pictures could create a visual joke, or add to the original one-liner, then by all means mention them. A standard layout is given in Figure 14.3.

There is a wide variety of humour ranges, from the whimsical and twee, to toilet humour and the risqué, and you will need to make sure you submit

N.E. Writer
Any Road
Anytown
Tel: 000-000

**Birthday caption 29 – Recycled**

(Pg 1)      It's important to be environmentally friendly
            (PICTURE – COUNTRYSIDE)

(Pg 3)      So here's a recycled birthday card
            Happy Birthday to
            (SERIES OF NAMES – JOHN, PETER,
            SAMANTHA, IAN, SARAH, ALL
            CROSSED THROUGH)

## Figure 14.3  Layout for a greetings card submission

to the right range. Request any writer's guidelines which are available and study the ranges available in card shops.

Submit ideas in batches of around ten or less at a time and be aware that seasonal material is usually required many months in advance.

---

**EXERCISES**

**1** Take several photographs from newspapers or magazines and write humorous captions for these.

**2** Take several printed spot cartoons and try to get new gags by writing different captions for the pictures, or describe different pictures for the same caption.

**3** Take a short humorous newspaper story and turn it into an eight-frame picture strip story. You will need to establish the key points of the story and decide how to visualize them. Make sure you stick to the story without invention or contrivance.

# 15 | ANIMATION

Animation is not just about cartoons that move, and it is not just for children. New technology is reducing the tediousness of a lot of the production processes of animation and with the success of *The Simpsons* has come the animated sitcom and cartoons for all ages: *King of the Hill*, *South Park*, *Beavis and Butthead*, *Ren and Stimpy*, *Rug Rats* and *Stressed Eric*.

The future for animation looks bright and in an economically aware media industry, animation has the advantages of greater sales potential in worldwide markets, as a sound track can easily be dubbed over in a foreign language.

The written script in the production of a piece of animation is only one part of the process. The script then goes to a storyboard stage, there are artists, model constructors, set makers and a whole crew of film makers involved.

In the early days of animation there were no writers, only storyboard artists. As the process has become more sophisticated and complex and animation has extended into feature film length, there has been a greater need for narrative, structure and dialogue, which has led to increased specialization.

## Why use animation?

> Animation must begin where reality ends, and its best sources are
> stories from out of this world, the world of fantasy and imagination.
>
> John Halas in *Masters of Animation*

The visual challenges of animation are immense and there are also challenges of characterization as life is given to shapes, solid objects, animals, buildings – in fact anything.

As with comic strip there is no set which is too expensive or exotic; there is no stunt which is too difficult. The scientific laws of physics, biology and chemistry are no restriction either. You have all the advantages of comic strip with the bonus of being able to make them move and add sound and music.

It is no coincidence that animation is used in human engineering, design analysis, scientific studies, simulated training, experimenting with aerodynamic and physical concepts, educational packages, TV title sequencing, even moving symbols on weather maps – there is no other way these effects could be achieved.

# Types of animation

## Stop motion or drawn animation

Drawn animation is used, for example, in Disney films and Tom & Jerry. The method used is to draw individual frames which are then filmed with a special camera which can record one or more frames at a time, rather than running continuously. For each frame the background and characters are moved slightly so when the film is completed there will be the effect of movement.

> The control of speed is the essence of animation.
>
> Richard Taylor in
> *The Encyclopaedia of AnimationTechniques*

As there are 25 frames per second on a video recording, 24 frames on film, something as simple as the raising of an eyebrow can take many drawings, while a five-minute animation may take as many as 7,500 drawings. Instead of filming single frames, action can be speeded up by exposing the film for two or three frames, however, movement will be marginally less fluid.

An industry method of production is generally used with the characters and backgrounds standardized so that different people can work on the drawings. Line drawings are the easiest to standardize.

## Claymation (aka model animation)

Small three-dimensional models are constructed and jointed, covered with a plasticine which is unaffected by studio lighting, and moved minutely by hand for each frame.

Some points on model animation:

- Keep sets to the minimum. Scaled down sets have the advantage of allowing the camera to view the set and characters from different angles, but are costly and time-consuming to make.
- Keep costume changes to the minimum. Again, they are costly and time-consuming to make.
- Avoid body and walking movements. The range of body movement is limited and as models are inclined to topple over when in walking poses, they need to be supported by pinning or magnetizing the feet.
- Subtlety of facial expressions is limited as a different head needs to be made for each expression.
- Continuity is sometimes a problem as once a model has been moved it is difficult to reshoot the scene exactly as it was.

With visual variety limited, story and characterization are all important for claymation.

## Computer animation

Computers are revolutionizing animation and when still images are scanned into a computer they can be coloured, or moved digitally, so saving immense amounts of time on individual drawings. Computers can also generate images and shapes, while characters and their movements can be viewed from any angle.

Animation is now available to anyone with a multimedia computer system, as there are software packages with standard backgrounds and characters that help with storyboarding and the drawing and importing of images, characters, locations and props. There are also packages for everything from planning and budgeting through to final production.

## Cut-out animation

Two-dimensional characters are made with separate limbs. Characters are then pinned on a board and moved for each frame. There is much less fluidity of movement and quicker, slapstick movements work better. This method can more easily be done by a single person.

## Other forms

Images scraped out of sand, painted on glass, or scratched out of exposed but undeveloped film, can all be used in animation. It does need to be precise and it is impossible to go back and re-do an image if a mistake is made.

These forms of animation lend themselves less easily to lengthy projects and bigger production teams and are often short works created by individuals.

## Mixed media

*Who Framed Roger Rabbit* was the first feature length film to combine live action and animation throughout, while *The Mask* used live action and cartoon-style animation blended with computer technology.

# The components of an animation story

## Characters

Characters should be worked out as fully and three dimensionally as with any other form of writing, however there are some differences as characters are brought to life not by actors, but by an artist or model maker who will design the character. They create a unique personality through physical size and proportions, eye and mouth movements, hand and body behaviour, style of movement, mannerisms and clothing.

Characters need to have an unambiguous, stronger and clearer personality than a live action or even a picture story script, as artists will need to convey a character visually through actions and expressions which can be exaggerated.

The temperament of a character has to be shown through what they do, and the maxim 'show, don't tell' applies more than ever to animation. Eric of *Stressed Eric* for instance, has a vein which throbs in his head when he is stressed – a visual way of showing his anxiety.

An artist will need to be able to imagine not just what the characters do, but how they do it. Give enough character introduction for this, leaving room also for artistic interpretation.

As animation is time-consuming, extra work and thought needs to go into devising characters in the pre-production stages and it is sensible to keep the number of characters to a minimum. (See also Chapter 10, Sitcom 2 – Devising sitcom characters.)

## Dialogue

In animation, dialogue holds the story up and should therefore be brief.

Keep speeches short: animated characters cannot act as well as real people and the range of facial expressions cannot be as subtle. Long speeches also involve fiddly decisions on how to vary the pictures.

## The storyboard

The storyboard is the visual interpretation of the script and consists of a series of screens with pictures of what will be seen, together with information on dialogue and sound.

A storyboard will show the shaping of the action and scene changes in the script. Additionally, it will show the style of the show and indicate the flow of the story. Artists will develop the storyboard into individual frames.

On smaller scale projects a writer can include stick drawings to give an idea of the sequences. Perhaps more so than with a comic strip script, room has to be left for visual interpretation. The important thing is to be clear about the visual aspects which are essential for the story or the joke.

Both the storyboard and the script become the blueprints for everyone working on the show, with the director making more use of the storyboard as the show develops visually. Voice artistes will have a greater reliance on the script for their dialogue.

## The script

There is no standardized animation script layout and you will need to enquire as to whether a particular company has a preferred layout. Often a screenplay layout will be used, or a video layout with visuals in a left-hand column and sound in a right-hand column. The three-column layout in Figure 15.1 differentiates between dialogue, sound and action. Standard presentation as mentioned in Chapter 3 still applies.

| DIALOGUE | SOUND | ACTION |
|---|---|---|
| JOE: (FRIGHTENED)<br>You want me to go<br>in there? | Teeth clattering. | Joe's teeth clatter,<br>break, and fall out. |
| SUE: It's only a crèche | | Two shot, Sue and<br>a toothless Joe. |

## Figure 15.1  Animation script layout

There will be more stage directions in an animation script as the writer is also something of a director. Description of camera angles, zooms, close-ups, cuts, fades, and so on, will all need to be written into the script so they can be drawn up by the artist. You will need to describe each frame of action, if that is relevant to the story.

Description should be explicit and detailed: if something isn't mentioned, it won't be drawn up. If writing animation for children you should be especially responsible, for example, if children are shown riding bikes, they should be wearing a helmet, if they are riding in a car, they should use seat belts. Instructions to draw these would need to be included in a script.

Visual humour should take precedence over verbal humour.

Characters can be distorted into all sorts of shapes and sizes, have incredible and outrageous things happen to them and still survive. Instructions will need to indicate how they can be represented visually, in a way which is true to the character.

To develop a sense of timing and visualization it is a good idea to close your eyes and mentally run the pictures through your mind.

Any description should be brief and concise. Scripts should not be filled with flowing narrative and irrelevant description. Be careful of using analogies, for example, becomes as small as a mouse, as an artist may unintentionally characterize this as a mouse with tail and whiskers. It is better to say 'shrinks' if that is what you mean.

For each frame you will need to indicate:

- which characters are there.
- which characters are entering or leaving the frame.
- the actions and movements taking place.
- transitions such as wipes, fades, dissolves and cuts.
- essential props and any background props needed for a particular joke. Point out if they are to be moved, for example, roof tiles clatter and sparks fly from a character's rear end as he slides down a roof.
- locations.

For drawn animation, following action from different angles will involve further drawings, so aim to keep the same viewpoint, that is avoid changing from front to back, side, higher or lower views just for the sake of it.

The background location can be described generally, for example, mountainous, a deep gorge, cliff top, dingy neighbourhood, suburban neighbourhood. Be specific only when it is necessary to the story or joke.

## Facial expressions

It is difficult to synchronize dialogue with movements of the mouth and lips, and the movements will look odd if later the animation is dubbed over with a foreign language dialogue. Rather than never showing the face of a speaker, do this sparingly and make use of one of the many devices for off-screen dialogue, such as:

- using a voiceover.
- showing the listener's reactions.
- showing the speaker's eyes or the back of the head.
- using a long shot of characters at a distance.
- showing characters walking side on as they speak.
- giving a character a catchphrase or regular exclamation so the same drawings can be used many times, for example Homer Simpson's 'Doh!'
- facial responses, for example, surprise or anger, which are easier to do and make it seem we are looking at the characters as they talk.

The emotion in a piece of dialogue should be evident but, unlike drama, animation requires more actor's instructions such as (ANGRILY), (PUZZLED), (BEWILDERED) so that an artist will know to represent that emotion visually.

The action column of a script should indicate if the emotion is to be portrayed in a particular way. For example, anger could be portrayed as steam coming out of ears, the character could turn into a raging bull, or have a bulging red face.

## ⇨ **To market**

There are opportunities for narrative animation in children's and adult TV series and films of various lengths. A TV series will need to have the same sustainability as a sitcom and you will need to send a similar proposal package of script, synopsis, character outlines and further episode stories, in much the same way. A storyboard, stick drawing or otherwise, may be included. (See also Chapter 11, Sitcom 3 – To market.)

Use listings guides to find out what animation is currently available and watch the output to gain names of the production companies. Market reference books can then be used to gain contact details. An initial enquiry should be made asking if that company would be interested in looking at ideas and/or scripts and how these should be presented.

---

**EXERCISES**

**1** Record a televised animation and, concentrating on a two-minute segment, write the script you think would have accompanied this.

**2** Without using dialogue, write a short slapstick routine for animation. It does not have to be realistic. You will need to think of each action and what the result of that action will be, in effect, what happens. This will test your abilities to give concise instructions and to think in visual terms. Use a stick drawings storyboard if this helps.

# 16 | HUMOUR FOR FICTION AND NON-FICTION

Humorous fiction and non-fiction is in great demand by editors and publishers, but it is important to appreciate the difference between humour and comedy. While the concern of comedy is with punchlines, jokes and laugh out loud funnies, humour has a light-hearted touch and may raise no more than a smile in a reader.

All the comedy techniques mentioned in Chapter 4 are still available when writing with humour, but should be used with a lighter, more subtle touch. Word plays enjoy a much better status in humour.

## Observation

Being a good observer of life is a great asset to a humour writer. While character and life itself provide the pot for humour, it is the small and insignificant details which provide the ingredients for the pot. See how detail (and a somewhat tongue-in-cheek deference) has given a touch of humour to the following extract from a news report:

> The queue waiting to receive Lady Thatcher's signature snaked through china, silverware, kitchen utensils, computers, CDs, radio and TV and finally into the red-carpeted book department. There Lady Thatcher's right hand brandished a Papermate over the title pages of as many copies of her memoirs as she could yomp through.

> Penny Wark, *Today* newspaper

Become a keen, non-judgemental observer of life. Soak up the atmosphere of places and their people, look for life's incongruities, idiosyncrasies, oddities and foibles, and think of ways in which these can be portrayed to humorous effect.

# Tools and devices for humour

You may be writing a short story, a novel, a feature article for a magazine or newspaper and while they each have their own forms and constructions, you will be able to use the same tools and devices for applying humour.

## The antithetical technique

There is a humour writing maxim which says, 'write funny things straight, and straight things funny.' This means that if you have an ordinary situation which is not funny in itself, you write in a style which is humorous, and vice versa.

For example, the Sue Townsend novel, *The Queen and I* has a premise of the Queen going to live in that most disparaged of working class abodes – the council flat. The incongruity of the situation is funny in itself, and Sue Townsend gains the most humour by writing about the situation in a very matter-of-fact way.

Reversing the process, an ordinary situation such as God passing on the Ten Commandments to Moses, could be written humorously as shown by the extract from the following article. It talks of engraving on stone:

> … which by today's standards is quite slow technology … (which is the reason why) … God's 167 convoluted policy points … (and) carefully obscure fiscal and penal notions were sharpened into a brief résumé and given the catchy title of the Ten Commandments.
>
> Miles Kington, *From God To Moses, Off The Record*

Note how the humour develops from the incongruity of the language of modern day business world being transposed to biblical times.

## Style of writing

The antithetical technique can also be applied to the style of writing. A satirical or sarcastic touch can be given to a mundane situation, topic or person, by writing in a tone which is upbeat, bright and lively:

> I love Monday mornings! The chance to check that nobody has stolen your unfinished invoices, to check that reduced heating is still keeping the overheads down, and bliss of bliss, to be secure in the knowledge that the coffee machine still gives a nice, hot cup of brown sludge.

In the following extract, exaggeration and understatement have been used to describe how a television series is made:

> It all begins a long time ago when the Writer – she is an irritable person with bitten nails – gets a Red Telephone Bill. This sets the Writer thinking, and not so long later she has written a television series!
>
> Victoria Wood, Introduction to, *Mens Sana in Thingummy Doodah*

Note how upper case letters give an added sense of importance to the words 'Writer' and 'Red Telephone Bill', while the amount of time and energy which must be involved in writing a television series is reduced to 'not so long later.'

## Use of language

(See also Chapter 2, The Nature of Comedy – Cultural reference points.)

> Words are chameleons, which reflect the colour of their environment.
>
> Learned Hand

Humour writers should not only use funny sounding words, they should use the full descriptive and visual power of the written word.

> When I see a spade I call it a spade.
>
> Cecily in *The Importance of Being Earnest,* by Oscar Wilde

A spade, for instance, could more humorously be described as a child's worm chopper, a lazy gardener's nightmare, or a road worker's means of support during working hours.

Whether you are talking about stick insect fashion models, the well-furnished executive briefcase, the expensive nourishment served in restaurants, or that rarity, the dribble-free baby, words with humorous connotations, misused words, humorous turns of phrase, metaphor and simile, are all useful tools in the humorists hands.

Also make full use of visual imagery in description, and again, words and phrases which are antithetical to the subject or object will work well. If they say something truthful, then they will work even better.

## Truth

When we smile at something which is humorous, we do so because we can relate to the point being made, or we recognize the situation as telling us something which is all part of the human condition and human nature.

## Pace and rhythm

Punctuation in humorous writing is as important for giving pace and rhythm as it is for one-liners. For humour writing, however, punctuation, along with sentence constructions, can not only be used to give pace and rhythm to humour, but also to create humour in itself. This example, taken from an anecdotal article on daughters, shows how this can be done. The article first talks about sons:

> Mess? Yes. Plastic hand grenades trodden into your beautiful Wilton? You bet! Weekly trips to the local casualty department to get their fingers, toes and/or noses stitched back on? Regular as clockwork.

Daughters, on the other hand, are different …

> I'm proud to say that after seven years of tantrums (me), sobbing (them) and caving in under pressure (me again), I've finally solved the clothes problem. They choose, I pay.

Melanie Moore, *A Hair Raising Issue*

You will be able to see how short sentences have given this piece a lively pace. It then follows that long sentences and elaborate words would slow the pace down. Notice how the last line follows the timing of comedy, to become the equivalent of a punchline.

## Humorous characters

For non-fiction writing the antithetical technique can be used when writing about real people. Be careful, however, that you do not make anyone look too foolish. Taking truth as your benchmark, avoid causing offence, and steer clear of defamation and libel.

For works of fiction, characters can have similar qualities to comedy characters or could be quite extreme and zany. However, the further characters or situations stray from our expectations of what is considered normal and rational behaviour, the more unrealistic they become. This is fine so long as you have studied your market and know your surreal or off-the-wall submission will fit requirements.

# ⇨ **To market**

## Short stories

Market reference books will give information on many outlets for short stories including magazines, small press publications, audio cassettes and radio.

When writing fiction for spoken word outlets, think of the person who is going to have to read the story and avoid tongue twisters, sibilance and difficult to pronounce words. The use of contractions – can't, not cannot; won't, not would not – will make for a more natural sounding reading. A short story for spoken word should be a narrative with little or no dialogue.

It is usual to submit a fully written story which should be typed, double spaced, on one side of A4 white paper and have a cover sheet as shown in Figure 16.1. Enclose a stamped addressed envelope with all submissions.

```
                              N.E. Writer
                              Any Road
                              Anytown
                              Tel: 000-000




                         TELLING IT AS IT IS
                                 by
                            N.E. WRITER




                         Approx 1000 words
```

**Figure 16.1  Short story cover sheet**

## Non-fiction articles

Not all subjects will be suitable for humorous interpretation, so you will need to be sure the subject you are writing about will not be trivialized by humour. Articles which need to be objective and factual are less suitable for humorous interpretation.

Subjects which allow for more personal and individual interpretation are more suitable and include: anecdotal personal experience articles; reviews; travel articles; columns and much informational and educational material. The humour in non-fiction writing should not detract from the subject you are writing about, rather it should make it more interesting.

## Novels/non-fiction books

Market reference books will help with finding a publisher for novels or non-fiction books. For the latter you can make an initial inquiry to a publisher to see if they would be interested in a book on the subject you wish to write about.

With both fiction and non-fiction it is not usual to submit the whole book, but to send a proposal package which should consist of:

- a covering letter – think of this as a selling document and promote the best points of the book, and suggest why it will be a publishing asset. For memoirs, autobiographies and personal life stories you will need to say why this should be of interest to other people.
- a synopsis of the book – a non-fiction book should also have chapter outlines.
- details of your experience and qualifications for writing on that subject for non-fiction books.
- three sample chapters.
- a stamped addressed envelope.

---

**EXERCISES**

1 Write a 500-word humorous review of an episode of a TV soap opera of your choice.
2 Write a humorous anecdotal story of around 1,000 words on a hobby or interest which you have. Ask your local radio station if they would be interested in broadcasting this.
3 Write a short humorous story for a magazine of your choice.

# 17 | WRITING COMEDY FOR CHILDREN

Comedy can be written for children ranging in ages from one or two years old, right up to age 16, although 12 and upwards is increasingly becoming defined as 'young adults'.

The toughest of critics, children are not small-sized adults, neither are they babies. Fail to write to their viewpoint and they will certainly let you know you have got things wrong.

## Writing *for* children, not *about* them

There are really no tricks to writing for children, it's simply a matter of writing with the child in mind and from the child's point of view.

Lois Lowry, children's writer

When writing for children it is not enough to have a child as the central character: stories need to be told from a child's point of view, and that is very different from an adult's point of view. Children do not see themselves as cute, charming or always noisy and argumentative, neither do they see adults as always right, wise and knowledgeable.

*Oliver Twist* has a child as the main character, but is not written for children: the language, the depth of emotions and concepts used all make it a book for adults. On the other hand, Mark Twain's *Huckleberry Finn* and *Tom Sawyer*, the *Just William* books of Richmal Crompton, and Dorothy Edwards's *My Naughty Little Sister* books have real-life characters, getting into real-life scrapes with which children can identify.

Be sensitive to children rather than sentimental.

When writing for children you will also need to be aware that the world of today's children is very different from that of your own childhood. Children today have different influences and interests, have a greater affinity with modern technology, are better informed and can handle concepts and ideas more easily than their parents did at the same age.

Stories today do not always have to be safe and cosy, they can be more challenging and many subjects which were once taboo are now being tackled quite openly. Comedy and humour are an ideal medium for making more difficult topics accessible, providing it is done with sensitivity, responsibility and with relevance to the age group of the intended audience.

# Special considerations

## Best kinds of comedy to use

In real life, children are always being told how the world behaves, and how they should behave. Anything which goes against this trend will be funny by being incongruous.

The bizarre, the zany, slapstick and the just plain silly or ludicrous, objects and people that do not behave as expected, all provide a springboard for the imaginative use of comedy.

Daft definitions, puns, riddles, crazy song and book titles, knock-knock jokes and all kinds of word play work well. When children are in the processes of learning to express themselves vocally, words and language are toys to be played with.

Satire, sarcasm and irony are not good comedy for children. The political and social machinations which underpin satire are outside the range of most children's experience, while sarcasm and irony can be too subtle for children.

## Characters

Funny characters for children's works are people who get things wrong or are accident-prone, children who buck real life by doing things children would not normally do, so long as it is not immoral or criminal, and children who are naughty, so long as they are not vindictive or nasty. Loved are grown-ups who are stupid, particularly if they are of that dreaded breed of spoilsports – either a teacher or a parent. Children like this reversed superiority and power hierarchy between adults and children, but it should be done responsibly.

Dotty, daft, dopey characters, muddlers and totally batty and foolish characters are liked by younger children, but can be seen as ridiculous and childish by older children. Up to about teenage years, characters can be more over the top, sillier and stupider.

The main character for any children's work should always be a child or children, who solve their own problems and get themselves out of scrapes, and do not have some adult do it for them. Main characters should be of an age which is towards the older end of the intended age range. Children of six don't mind reading about children aged nine, but not the other way a round.

## Adults buy, children consume

The peculiarity in writing for children is that it is adults who commission the material to be broadcast, published or performed, and adults who decide what children watch on TV, and who buy the books children read.

As ever, there will be some disagreements as to what is good and bad for children, but a writer has to remember that young minds are easily influenced and distorted. The younger the child being written for, the greater the moral and ethical restrictions that will apply.

## Responsibility

> The juvenile writer carries an additional responsibility in his work, for he is dealing with a young mind, one that is emerging and shaping.
>
> Roy E Porter

It is not considered appropriate for badness to triumph, nor is it appropriate to glorify self centredness, cruelty, greed, materialism and other negative emotions. Honesty, kindness and generosity should be shown as positive attributes, while also recognizing that they are sometimes hard to achieve if, for instance, you are a child having to share a bedroom with an annoying sibling.

The younger the child, the greater should be the distinctions between fantasy and reality, and good and bad. Everything should be clearly black or white, as young children in particular are not able to handle or understand grey areas. This does not mean you should be moralistic or preachy, but that you should show through example that bad is wrong and good is right.

Think always of the values you are promoting: make them always positive images and positive values.

There are arguments, however, which say that more realistic and scarier stories can help children to work through their fears. It is certainly true that humour can be instrumental in helping children cope: a wicked witch, for instance, is not so scary if she is funny.

## Language

Reading books and stories is part of a child's education so it is important that grammar and syntax are correct. This does not mean you cannot use devised words, for younger children this works very well, or that you cannot use colloquialisms and other expressions, as these can give life to a story. Contractions are used in everyday speech and can make a narrative sound more friendly. It is a case of knowing the rules before you can break or bend them, and knowing the reasons why you are breaking them.

Bad language (swearing) is not considered appropriate for children's works but this has to be balanced when writing for young adults as it is very much part of their world. It should be used with discretion, and only when necessary.

## Research

As with any other medium or form of comedy writing you need to know your audience and a lot of this research will have already been done for you. Television departments ask children for opinions on programmes, libraries have literature on children's books, newspapers and magazines have reviews and profiles of children's books and television programmes, and literature on teaching will give guidelines and information about the good and bad in resources for children.

It would be nice to say you should concentrate on past masters and the classics of children's literature and television, however it is more important to find out what children like today and to get a feel for what is being commissioned *now*. Read children's books and comics, watch children's TV and be non-judgemental.

Once you have a feel for what is around, you should not then aim to manufacture a book to some formulaic common denominator. Aim for original and fresh angles on current trends, and to write something which reflects the world of today's children convincingly.

# Age groups

While mostly a marketing tool, age group ranges are used by parents and those who sell children's works to help with assessment of appropriateness. It is important when submitting material for children to state the intended age group.

## Pre-school age group

> Remember how minutely observant and noticing small children are.
>
> Joan Aitken

Very young children are interested in the small things of everyday life – making sandwiches, a spider in the bath, a bus or train journey, multicoloured ice cream or a dog with a droopy ear.

> I think in poems you try to pick words which don't just have meaning but which have sounds and pictures attached to them.
>
> Liz Lochhead

Children of this age enjoy books with a lot of visual content, whether that is in pictures or words, poetry or prose which conjures up mental pictures.

Liked also are lots of repetition and funny and strange-sounding words, anything with rhythm or rhyme – songs, poems, jingles – the words themselves not being so important as the melody and any actions which can accompany the words.

Short, straightforward, simple stories of the bedtime or fairytale variety are always popular. These should be stories with simple sentences, easy-to-follow action and a definite beginning, middle and a happy ending. They should involve situations and events recognizable to the child, for example, family life and everyday experiences. A child at this age is still trying to make sense of the world and is not always able to distinguish between fiction and reality, so be aware that they may interpret things literally.

Younger children especially need to feel loved and secure. Seeing or reading about children, especially of their own age, getting hurt, humiliated or victimized can be frightening so you will need to think carefully about the use of slapstick and practical jokes.

## Five- to eight-year-old age group

Stories can be longer and situations can be more realistic, for example, having arguments, feeling stupid or being shy. There can be more depth of character and the older end of this age group may be able to appreciate cause and effect (action and reaction) and have a greater understanding of concepts of sadness, happiness, being scared, being sorry.

There should still be a clear distinction between good and bad and although children can be naughty, they should also be reprimanded.

## Nine- to 12-year-old age group

Stories can now involve more complex emotions and plots. Plot should be watertight, interesting and have a strong pace. Children have a short attention span and as soon as the action starts to drag they will go and do something else.

Characters should be three-dimensional and non-stereotypical. Bad language should be avoided, as should innuendo and immoral or illegal activities.

## Over 12 years age group

Teenagers' interests are many and varied – relationships, personal appearance, spots, developing independence, being misunderstood, the pressures of schoolwork, environmental issues, protest, clothes, music and so on.

There is a big market for young adults' books on relationships and serious subjects, but few, if any, have been written with humour. The area is more difficult but perhaps there is a gap waiting to be filled?

# Outlets for children's writing

## Short stories and novels

Some magazines for children and young adults use short stories, and you should consult market reference books to find which these are.

There is a much bigger demand for humorous fiction novels for children than for adults. Consult market reference books for names of publishers and browse through bookshops to see what is currently available.

## Illustrations

As a general guide, the younger the child the greater the amount of illustrative matter.

There are no rules about whether a manuscript (ms) should be submitted with illustrations or not. A publisher will often find an artist, but you could team up with an artist and submit a book as a complete package. The only guideline is that the illustrations should be top quality.

An artist does need visual imagery which lends itself to illustration and the written words should give rise to pictures at regular intervals.

> The flowers were sweetly singing, The birds were in full bloom.
>
> From *Twas In The Month Of Liverpool*, Anon

You will see how the above rhyme extract leads very easily and imaginatively to illustration. Daffodils could be drawn trumpeting a melody, or a spike of flowers shown with ascending notes. If you have ideas for illustration, these can be suggested to an artist.

## Poetry

From nursery rhymes onwards, children like rhythm and rhyme, if it is also funny it will be enjoyed even more. Perhaps not always worthy of being called 'proper poetry' rhythm and rhyme helps children to become more versatile with words and language, and makes the gaining of memorizing skills more fun.

To distance themselves from the babies, slightly older children, maybe with some reading ability of their own, can appreciate distorted nursery rhymes – using the 'twisted cliché' comedy technique to change the last line of a nursery rhyme to give a surprise ending or twist the whole rhyme, as Lewis Carroll did with 'Twinkle, Twinkle Little Bat'. Limericks, riddles, funny sounding and invented words can all be used.

Blank verse that is funny is difficult as the standard gag construction of straight line and punchline has a rhythm of its own and it may look as though you are merely passing off gags as blank verse. Make the rhythm much stronger and make it rhyme.

Consult market reference books to find a suitable publisher for your work.

## Television

Most countries have many hours of dedicated children's programming; and sitcoms, comedy drama and comedy inserts to light entertainment programmes are always welcomed. For current requirements contact the Youth and Entertainment or Children's Department of broadcasters or production companies. Although not a big market for original material, there are several satellite channels providing solely children's programming. (See also Chapter 14, Cartoon and comic strip and Chapter 15, Animation.)

Family orientated and across age range programming is much in demand, as this can be a means of being economical without lowering standards.

## Radio/audio cassettes

Whereas in the past radio was a popular medium for children's entertainment, the advent of TV and video have drastically lessened the demand. However, there are still opportunities for entertaining children by use of audio cassettes. Consult market reference books for further information.

## Children's entertainers

Comedians, ventriloquists, magicians and others who provide children's entertainment at holiday camps, for seasonal shows and children's parties, may require jokes, anecdotes, stories and scenarios which they can develop.

Research a performer's act in the same way you would a stand-up comedian. Whether writing for an individual entertainer or providing a package have a variety of material for different ages and different occasions.

Children's entertainers may advertise for material in entertainment magazines and newspapers or you could advertise your services in the same places, or make a personal approach in the same way as for a stand-up comedian. (See also Chapter 13, Stand-up comedy – Contacting comedians.)

# Children's theatre

The first consideration when writing plays or other performance entertainment for children, is whether you intend children to be the watchers (audience) or the players (cast).

Works for children to watch include performances in a theatre setting, Theatre in Education (TIE) and short works for performance in museums and other venues.

# Theatre for children to watch

## Theatre venues

Children's theatre does have something of a Cinderella status but there are nevertheless a few dedicated children's theatres: others may include children's works in their programme and children's plays can be staged in community and church halls, arts centres and other venues. Humour is especially sought in children's theatre as it is very efficient in keeping wriggly and disruptive children interested and entertained.

Aim for a total running time of around an hour and keep the pace and level of interest high. Having something happening all the time and incorporating music, dance and movement are means of ensuring children stay interested and entertained.

It is best not to target a theatrical work at too narrow an age range as this will have the effect of reducing the number of people wanting to watch it, which will then increase the ecomonic risk of staging that work. Aim for either younger (four to eight) or older children (nine to mid teens) and have something with an appeal for all children, or a family orientated show. (See also Chapter 12, Theatre.)

## Theatre in Education (TIE)

Taking a theatrical piece into schools, not merely for entertainment but for its education value, is the mainstay of many a theatre company. Again, humour is a very effective tool in getting facts across in an entertaining way.

TIE is rarely just the performance of a straight script: it may be acted out along with improvisation and other interaction with the children; or it may involve question and answer sessions to discuss aspects of the company's work, or issues raised by the play. Be prepared to write all the accompanying material if necessary.

Short scripts may be a dramatization of an historical event or era, the life of a famous person, life in a different culture or country. Older children may appreciate a playlet on a topical issue such as crime, bullying or relationships.

Contact theatre companies to see if they do TIE work and consult market reference books, theatre resource centres, and arts centres for information on TIE groups. You may also be able to contact schools directly with scripts for reading or acting out in class. Invite teachers and educationists to a performance of the script so they can see before they buy.

# Theatre for performance by children

## The school play

Often giving children their first taste of acting, the school play can be a published script, an improvisation, or be devised and written by a teacher, perhaps being added to during rehearsals. The school play may also be a script written specially, often for seasonal, celebratory, end of term performances or to enhance curriculum studies.

Schools' resources and facilities may often be limited, so keep sets, props and costume simple. A simple backdrop which can suffice for all scenes is all that is required. Forests and gardens are good locations for younger children as several children can play the parts of trees, flowers, and so on.

A running time of around 30–45 minutes is adequate for children aged four to seven as they take longer to rehearse and their audiences may include very young brothers and sisters, who will not be able to concentrate for longer. Plays for older children may be longer.

Dialogue should be short, simple and easy to learn with clear cues and a logical progression of cause and effect, which will make learning lines easier.

Movements, actions, entrances and exits have to be learnt too, and for younger children in particular, these should relate to the dialogue where possible. A line which says, 'I've got a magic sword that'll get rid of dragons, I'll go and get it' leads clearly to a child knowing they then have to exit.

The older the children, the more demanding may be the dramatic content and the depth of characterization. For children over the age of 11 plays which deal with the issues and concerns of older children are useful for their learning and discussion content. Humour should be handled carefully and the issues should never be trivialized or demeaned.

## Youth theatre, drama workshops and courses

There may not be so many opportunities here as devised dramas are common. Nevertheless, you may find a home here for plays which reflect the lives of children of various ages and allow for the development of acting skills. There is room for innovation and imagination and the plays do not always need to be centred on children. *Bugsy Malone* for instance, has adult characters intended to be played by children.

## Educational and non-fiction works

There is always room for humour in factual material as it will make learning easier and more fun. It is important to remember that humour is only a vehicle to carry the facts, and should not be used to distort them.

Textbooks, how-to and general interest books and articles for magazines, schools programmes for both radio, television and video, all provide outlets for non-fiction written with humour. Market reference books should be used to find details.

When writing educational material for use in schools, you must first research any curriculum requirements, information on which can be found in libraries or by contacting schools directly. If you wish to write material for schools in other countries the principle remains the same: research first.

---

**EXERCISES**

**1** Using the 'people, places, props' method of brainstorming (see Chapter 3) make lists which are within the range of experience of children aged between four and seven. Write a short story or poem involving three of these items, one from each column.

**2** Rewrite a traditional fairy story so it has a contemporary feel and is relevant to children aged between nine and 12 years of age.

**3** Devise a short original drama for 12- to 16-year-olds on a current topic.

# 18 THE BUSINESS OF BEING A COMEDY WRITER

To think of comedy writing in the cold, hard terms of a business may seem to be at odds with the inspirational nature of creativity.

If you want your comedy writing to be no more than a hobby, then it is fine to write only when you feel inspired or the mood takes you. If you want to be a successful comedy writer on a regular basis, however, you will be entering a highly competitive world in which you will need to be both businesslike and professional.

The successful comedy writer in this kind of world has to not only have the skill and talent to write good comedy, he or she must have the self-discipline and self-motivation to maintain work of the highest standard, on a regular basis.

## Marketing your work

### Tactics for success

There are simple tactics which will give you your best chances and reduce the risks of rejection.

- *Submit only your best work* Sending material which is sloppily written, or which has not been thought through properly, will only waste a reader's time and give you a bad reputation. It is better to send only a few good sketches than a big bundle of bad or mediocre ones.

- *Use the potentials of the medium* Whether you are writing for radio, TV, comic strip or whatever, know the strengths of the medium. Always ask if this could have been done on any other medium.

- *Make an initial impact* Script readers and editors do read all of a script or manuscript but can nevertheless evaluate it in the first few pages, or the first few lines for shorter works. Making these good, interesting and funny means the rest of the script will be read in a positive frame of mind. Remember too that if a script reader loses interest at the beginning, so will an audience.

■ *Have professional presentation*  This will be discussed in more detail later.

■ *Target your work appropriately*  The best comedy writing in the world will be rejected if it does not fit the market to which it is submitted. Research your markets and write to that market.

■ *Time the submission of work effectively*  If there is a deadline for a submission, try to get your work in well before the last-minute rush. A script reader will then have more time to consider your work, under less hectic conditions. Sketches submitted early in a TV production schedule give better chances, and often it is a case of 'first in, first accepted'.

## Tactics for increasing income

It is extremely difficult to make a full-time living from comedy writing but with a little ingenuity you may be able to increase your income:

■ *Adapt your work for other markets*  Always aim to find more than one market for a piece of work. One-liners can be adapted for many different outlets or developed into sketches; sketches can provide the basis for a short story or an anecdotal type article, or a piece of drama.

■ *Write about comedy*  For magazines and newspapers, you could write anecdotal articles about the life traumas and triumphs of being a comedy writer; reviews comedy shows and comedians, interview comedians and other comedy writers, or write articles and books on the craft of comedy writing.

■ *Run workshops and seminars*  In this way you can pass on your skills and experience to aspiring comedy writers. There are many course and seminar organizers who may be interested in including comedy writing in their programme and you only need to contact them with a workshop proposal. You may need to do this well in advance as programmes are often prepared a year ahead. Alternatively, you could organize a workshop or seminar yourself, arranging your own venue and publicity.

■ *Teach comedy writing* Colleges, universities and other learning or extracurricular establishments may include modules on comedy writing. You may need to prove you know your subject and/or have teaching skills.

## Keeping records – general points

It is not usual to resubmit work to the same market or show, but given the subjective nature of comedy, and changes of requirements and personnel in commissioning departments, a different person may view your work in a different light at a different time. You may then be able to resubmit on some occasions and you may find it useful for your records to contain a note of the person to whom you submitted the work.

There are various methods of record keeping, and you should choose whichever suits you best.

■ *File cards* with the title of the work, word length or running time and submission details are useful for keeping track of longer works but not very practical if you have hundreds of one-liners and sketches.

■ *A catalogue* of sketches and one-liners may be more useful. A copy of each sketch can be filed with submission details recorded on the same sheet. They can be filed by subject or topic and set/location.

■ *Databases* offer the most comprehensive means of record keeping and filing if you have the computer equipment and knowledge to use them.

# Marketing yourself

## Personal qualities

There are hundreds if not thousands of comedy writers and any producer or script editor will always choose to work with people who do not make their life difficult. Always be pleasant, courteous and professional. Be a good listener and a good team player. Appear confident, even if you don't feel confident. Don't be subservient, appeasing or sycophantic and never be pushy, argumentative, over-powering, temperamental, loud mouthed or aggressive. Being not just busy, but *very* busy, is the mark of anybody who works in any comedy writing medium, so always respect their time.

## Your reputation

Having a good reputation is everything in the comedy world so it is worthwhile building up a good one. Get yourself known for the quality of your work and, as always, be professional – deliver the goods, well presented, as asked for, and on time.

# Other business concerns

## Copyright

There are many books with detailed information on copyright so I will concentrate here on peculiar problems with copyright in connection with comedy.

With regard to formats, there are no copyright problems in using such as a Cinderella format, but you should be careful when parodying formats of radio, television and commercials. It is better to give a general impression of the distinguishing components of a format rather than copy them slavishly.

Duplication of sketches and one-liners can and does occur quite naturally. Topical material particularly suffers from a lot of duplication as writers are dealing with the same news items, and there is a finite number of connections which can be made: it's here that the writer who can find an alternative angle on topics will stand out.

Similarly, a writer's brief for a sketch show will result in many writers submitting similar or almost identical sketches, as writers will all be dealing with the same sets, locations and characters and there are only so many things that can happen in those places and to those characters.

When hundreds of sitcom scripts are received in television departments it is also likely many of them will be based on similar premises of contemporary interests. In America it is standard practice for scripts not to be read unless a release form has been signed. This releases the company from any charges of plagiarism should they be working on a similar idea and limits their liability in the event of legal action. Other countries, such as the UK, have no system of release forms and all unsolicited scripts are read.

It is easy to become a real worrier where copyright is concerned and you should keep in mind that any work which is kept hidden in a drawer for fear of theft, is work that is never going to be sold.

## Working as a freelance writer

Freelance writers are usually responsible for dealing with their own income tax payments and you should contact your local tax or revenue office for information and advice on freelance earnings and the system for payment of taxes. Often you will be able to offset certain allowances and expenses against your tax bill and you should keep accurate records of all monetary incoming and outgoing in connection with your work.

The *Writer's and Artist's Yearbook* and *Writer's Market* have basic information on tax systems in the UK and America respectively. Local libraries will often have leaflets and books available on taxation matters.

## Agents

The writer of short comedy or humorous material – sketches, lines, greetings cards, short stories, humorous articles, and so on – will find that even with an extensive track record, an agent may not be interested in representing them.

### Do you really need an agent?

Agents can find work for you, negotiate the best price for your work, provide introductions and handle contracts. They can also take a percentage of anything you earn, whether you find that work yourself or not.

Alternatives to agents are:

- Membership of the Writers' Guild or Society of Authors or similar organizations which act as a union for writers and will give help with legal information and advice. There are also lawyers who specialize in copyright and literary contracts.
- Attending conferences, seminars, workshops and courses, which will help with building up contacts.
- Joining a comedy writer's group or association can help build a network of contacts and, depending on the nature of the organization, enable you to gain feedback on your work.

- Keeping up to date with what is going on in the comedy world by reading comedy and general writing journals and magazines. Networking and talking to people will also help.
- Markets can be found through networking, joining relevant organizations, enquiry letters and phone calls, talking to people or following up leads, for example, a line in a newspaper that a particular comedian is going to make a new show, or a new independent production company is being formed.
- Making sure your work is always out and being seen will get your name known and raise your profile. If somebody is looking for a comedy writer, your name will then spring more easily to mind.

## Courses

Many countries have a wide range of media and writing courses at every level from hobby to Masters degrees. Courses do give opportunities to learn, improve and sharpen your skills, give you a kick-start to getting started, and course assignments do actually make you write. They are a way of meeting like-minded people, gaining valuable contacts and often gaining access to library, computer and other facilities and equipment. Residential courses are also an enjoyable working holiday. There are details of course and seminar organizers in the appendices. Alternatively consult market reference books, arts publications, writing magazines or educational institutions. You may also find out information on the internet.

However, while all knowledge and education is useful, you do not need to be qualified to write. No matter how highly educated or trained you are, in the end it is the standard and quality of the work submitted which matters most. You can teach someone how to be a gymnast, to play a sport or a musical instrument but it is the practise which makes perfect, and if you are a comedy writer you have to write comedy, and write on a regular basis.

# 19 | THE COMEDY WRITER AS A HUMAN BEING

## Motivation

It is not always easy for the writer working alone at home to find the self-motivation needed to maintain a continuous output of work. Many things can have an annoying habit of interfering with a writing day – writer's block, despondency after receiving a batch of rejected material, other commitments, more immediate concerns may steal time, or the sun may be shining and we would rather be outside than stuck at a keyboard. Any writer can find a 1001 reasons not to write.

Motivation and self-discipline often go together and setting yourself targets – yearly, monthly, weekly, depending on your kind of writing – will enable you to plan your workload, and give you something to aim for.

Targets need to be realistic and achievable rather than merely optimistic. Get to know your own work patterns, the average length of time it takes you to produce a piece of work, and adjust your targets if you find you are not making them on a regular basis.

## Time management

Whether you have a lot or a little time in which to write you may find that it becomes filled with a multitude of non-creative and time-wasting distractions, and small writing projects expand unnecessarily to fill the time available, particularly if you work from home. Some distractions can be eliminated by having an office or a dedicated room in the house where you can go as though to a workplace. If it is not possible to gain control over your place of writing in this way, you can still gain control over the time you have for writing.

Organizing your workload entails first recognizing the stages of producing a piece of work, which are:

1 Research. This may be market research, or assessing the requirements of a writer's brief.
2 Creative period of thinking/brainstorming.
3 Production period when the actual writing is done.
4 Rewriting and polishing period.
5 Submission of work and record keeping.

The stages are not always totally separate, or in that order. The important thing is to recognize the need for each and not to let administration take over from the creative and productive stages. A balance also has to be maintained between writing projects, business meetings, pitching sessions, networking and skill development. Prioritizing your workload and making lists will ensure you know what needs to be done and in which order.

Once you know what needs to be done, pre-plan your writing sessions so you can go straight into them.

Make writing a habit.

Establishing writing as a habit is something all writers should aim for, no matter how much or how little time they have. The routine of a regular work pattern can help reduce time spent on psyching yourself up to write, or time spent in sharpening pencils, tidying the desk or other delaying tactics needed to get in the right mood for writing.

Write a sketch a day, so when a market comes up you have always got something ready.

Ken Rock, President,
Comedy Writers Association UK

If you can, set aside a certain time each day when you know you will be able to write without interruption. If this is not possible, perhaps getting up an hour earlier or going to bed an hour later will enable you to find that extra time.

# Writer's block

Every writer goes through periods when they just cannot find anything to write about, or everything they do write seems to be substandard rubbish. Sometimes this may be the symptom of a loss of confidence, the fear of an approaching deadline or just tiredness.

Taking a rest may be all that is needed, or you could try one of the following devices:

- Just write anything: relaxing into the physical action and rhythm of writing can relieve anxiety and ease you into the writing you want to be doing.

- Go over what you have written in a previous session. Again, this eases you into the rhythm of writing.

- For a longer piece of work, leave it in the middle of a scene or chapter so at your next writing session you can pick up at a point where you already know what comes next.

- If you are stuck on a plot point, try bringing another character onto the scene, or take the action to another place. A different source of input to the action may get you over a sticking point.

- Let your subconscious do the work. Sleep on it, or go for a walk or a swim. The rhythm of physical activity can kickstart mental activity.

- Watch TV, listen to the radio, read a book, go for a drink with friends – you may find life itself, real or portrayed, can provide a solution or inspiration.

# Getting feedback

Ultimately, an audience is the only true judge of whether something is funny or not, but your work may need to pass through the hands of a lot of people before it can be presented to an audience.

Producers, editors and script editors often don't have time to give feedback: however, if you do get it, treasure it. Listen to what they have to say: you might not agree with their comments, but as gatekeepers, you do need to take the comments on board.

Friends, members of your family and colleagues can provide sources of initial feedback on your work but don't consider them a final authority on whether something is funny or not: they will know you and your sense of humour and will be a considerate audience in that they will not want to hurt your feeling or discourage you.

Feedback from other comedy writers is useful, as is working with other comedy writers. There are many writer's groups, a few specifically for comedy writers, or you could start one of your own. Call your local newspaper or ask your local library if they could put a notice up saying you are looking to form a comedy writers' group. Alternatively, you could join a professional comedy writer's organization (see Appendices).

There is also the DIY route: get together not only with writers, but actors or comedians and try out sketches or routines in an open mic spot at a comedy club. Even top name comedians will try their material out on smaller more informal audiences before using it for higher profile appearances.

Alternatively, many bars have a functions room which you may be able to use for free as any audience will bring increased bar receipts. Often you will be able to keep all the door money.

Or you could hire a theatre or other venue.

# Rejections

Rejections are part of any comedy writer's life, no matter how good they are. Writers of sketches and one-liners in particular can expect that a certain percentage of their material will not be taken up. As an example, one writer with a few mini-successes under his belt had the following 'hit rate' with a TV show:

> I sent in ten quickies ... They wrote back accepting two ... I sent in four more batches of ten. The final score was, they were interested in ten, and used five.

> Frank E Tennis

Rejections are not always justified and there are various reasons why submitted material may not be accepted, many of them having nothing to do with the quality of that material.

Producers may not be in the market for that kind of thing at the moment, have no room in the production schedules, may have enough sketches for that set, character or location, or have reached the full programme complement. There may be budgetary and other considerations of which you may not have been aware despite all your careful researches: decisions can change both rapidly and frequently.

Then there is always the subjective nature of comedy: it is all about individual and personal responses and another script reader could feel entirely different, even the same person can feel different at another time.

Material which is not taken up should not be seen as dead, however. It can be redirected or updated for another market. Lines, for instance, can be 'switched', turned into sketches, greetings cards or included in material for stand-up comedians, and vice versa.

Rejection should never be taken personally: send the material straight to another market and carry on with your next batch of sketches, or your next project.

## The luck factor

> We create our own good fortune.
>
> Gene Perret

There is always an element of luck in the opportunity that comes along through a chance meeting or being in the right place at the right time. There are, however, a lot of things you can do to increase the odds of a lucky chance coming your way.

- Perfect your skills and make sure your work is always the best quality you are capable of. Success never comes from badly written material and just one slipshod piece of work could close a door permanently. If a one in a million lucky chance does occur you will need good material to back it up.

- Research your markets well to ensure you get the right thing to the right person at the right time.

- Keep knocking on doors. If you knock on enough doors one of them will eventually open.

- Have a stock pile of material so that when an opportunity does come along you will be able to follow it up immediately.

- Seize every opportunity no matter how small. You can build on small successes and use them to open other doors.

- Always have your work out and being seen. Writers are known through their work so the more chance it has of being seen, the greater the chances of it being picked up. Even if a particular piece of work is not liked, your style may be, and this could lead to you being asked to write something else.

- Always have spec material available and be prepared to write on spec when necessary.

- ■ Let people know what you do, either informally and naturally when chatting, or formally by placing advertisements.
- ■ Don't just tell people what you do, show them. Compile a portfolio of your work. Don't, however, loan or leave it anywhere – things have a habit of getting lost.
- ■ Leave your CV and list of credits in as many places as you can, making sure it is always up to date.
- ■ Make a pilot recording and hawk it round.
- ■ Meet people, talk to people in the comedy writing business and follow up any leads which might provide an opportunity.

Do all of the above and you will not need to rely on luck. Always remember too, luck can never replace hard work and professionalism.

It is only left now to give you my very good wishes for future success and enjoyment of your comedy writing.

# APPENDICES

## Useful addresses

Note: When writing to any of the following it is courteous to enclose a stamped addressed envelope.

### Australia/New Zealand

Australian Broadcasting Corporation, GPO Box 9994, Sydney, NSW 2001 Australia.
 Tel: 02 9333 1500. Fax: 02 9333 5305. Web site: http://www.abc.net.au
Independent Theatre Association, Lotteries House, 79 Stirling Street, Perth,
 Western Australia 6000. Tel: 08 9220 0620. Fax: 08 9220 0617.
 Web site: http://cygnus.uwa.edu.au/~gmalcolm/ita/
Radio New Zealand Ltd., PO Box 2092, Wellington C1, New Zealand.
 Tel: 04 474 1555. Fax: 04 474 1340.
South Australian Writer's Circle, PO Box 43, Rundle Mall, Adelaide 5000, South
 Australia. Tel: 08 8223 7662. Fax: 08 8232 3994.
 Web site: http://www.sawriters
Television New Zealand Ltd., PO Box 3819, Auckland, New Zealand.
 Tel: 09 377 0630. Fax: 09 375 0918.

### North America

Canadian Broadcasting Corporation, 250 Lanark Avenue, PO Box 3220, Stn 'C'
 Ottawa, Ontario K1Y 1EA. Tel: 613 724 1200.
Copyright Public Information Office, Library of Congress, Washington DC
 20559, USA.
CTV Television Network, 250 Yonge Street, Suite 1800, Toronto, Ontario M5B
 2N8 USA. Tel: 416 595 4100.
National Association of Greetings Card Publishers, #330, 600 Pennsylvania Avenue,
 Washington DC 20003, USA.
Society of Children's Book Writers and Illustrators, 345 North Maple Drive,
 Suite 296, Beverly Hills, CA 90210, USA. Tel: 310 859 9887.
 Fax: 310 859 4877. e-mail: membership@scbwi.org
 Web site: http://www.scbwi/

## South Africa

African Writer's Association, Hampstead Building, Biccard Street, Braamfontein, 2001, South Africa. Tel: 011 403 2342.

Congress of South African Writers, PO Box 421007, Fordsburg, 2000, South Africa. Tel: 011 833 2530. Fax: 011 833 2532.

Magazine Publisher's Association of South Africa, PO Box 47184, Parklands, 2121, South Africa. Tel: 011 447 1264. Fax: 011 447 1289.

South African Broadcasting Corporation, Private Bag XI, Auckland Park, Johannesburg 2006, South Africa. Tel: 011 714 9111. Web site: www.sabc.co.za/

South African Writer's Circle, PO Box 10558, Marine Parade, Durban 4056, South Africa. Tel: 031 251769. Web site: http://www.lsgi.co.za/circle.htm

South African Scriptwriter's Association, PO Box 91937, Auckland Park 2006, South Africa. Tel/Fax: 011 678 0405.

## UK/Republic of Ireland

Association of Independent Radio Producers, Essel House, 29 Foley Street, London W1P 7LB, UK. Tel: 0171 323 2770.

BBC Comedy Script Unit, TV Centre, Room 4006, Wood Lane, London W12 7RJ, UK. Tel: 0181 743 8000.

BBC World Service, Bush House, PO Box 76, London WC2B 4PH, UK. Tel: 0171 240 3456. Fax: 0171 379 6729.

Cartoon Art Trust, Suite 40, Newhouse, 67–8 Hatton Garden, London EC1N 8JY, UK.

The Comedy Writers' Association UK, Ken Rock, President, 61 Parry Road, Ashmore Park, Wolverhampton, West Midlands WV11 2PS, UK. Tel/Fax: 01902 722729.

Greetings Card Association, 41 Links Drive, Elstree, Herts, WD6 3PP, UK. Tel: 0181 236 0024.

Performing Rights Society, 29–33 Berners Street, London W1P 4AA, UK. Tel: 0171 580 5544.

Radio Telefis Eireann, Donnybrook, Dublin 4, Republic of Ireland. Tel: 01 208 3111. Fax: 01 208 3080. Irish national radio and TV broadcaster.

## International Association of Writers Guilds:

Web site: http://www.wga.org/iawg/index.html

Australia: 60 Kellett Street, Kings Cross, NSW 2011, Australia. Tel: 02 9357 7888. Fax: 02 9357 7776. Web site: http//www.ozemail.com.au/~awgsyd/

Canada: 123 Edward Street, Suite 1225, Toronto, Ontario M5G 1E2, Canada. Tel: 416 979 7907.

New Zealand: PO Box 47886, Ponsonby, Auckland 1034, New Zealand.
   Tel: 649 373 2960. Fax: 649 373 2961.
South Africa: 37 17th Street, Parkhurst 2193, South Africa.
UK: 430 Edgeware Road, London W2 1EH, UK. Tel: 0171 723 8074.
USA (east): 555 W 57th Street, New York, NY 10019, USA. Tel: 212 767 7800
USA (west): 8955 Beverly Blvd., West Hollywood, Ca. 90048–2456, USA.
   Tel: 310 550 1000.

# Further reading

## Market reference books

*Animation UK* – (BECTU, London) Annual guide to animation personnel and
   production companies in UK and Europe.
*Blue Book of British Broadcasting, The* – Ed. R Mann (Tellex Monitors Ltd). Contact
   information for terrestrial, satellite and cable TV and radio.
*British Theatre Directory* – S Black, Editor (Richmond House Publishing Co. Ltd,
   London). Annual publication with contact information for theatres and theatre
   companies, comedy and cabaret venues, publishing.
*Children's Writer's and Illustrator's Market* (Writer's Digest, Cincinnati, Ohio).
   Annual reference source for American markets.
*Humor and Cartoon Market* (Writer's Digest, Cincinnati, Ohio). Annual reference
   source for American markets.
*Media Guide, The* (Guardian Books, London). Annual press and broadcast
   directory.
*Novel and Short Story Writer's Market* (Writer's Digest, Cincinnati, Ohio). Annual
   reference source for American markets.
*Book Writer's Handbook, The* – Gordon Wells (Allison & Busby, London).
   Published biennially. Information on book publishers and their lists.
*The Comedy Market: A Writer's Guide to Making Money and Being Funny* –
   Carmine De Sena (Berkley, New York, 1996).
*How to Get Published in South Africa* – Basil Van Rooyen (Southern Books,
   Bergvlei).
*Magazine Writer's Handbook, The* – Gordon Wells (Allison & Busby, London).
   Published biennially, detailed information on magazine requirements.
*World Radio, TV Handbook* – Ed. A G Sennith (Billboard Books). Available from:
   BPI Communications, 1515 Broadway, New York 10036, USA and Windsor
   Books International, The Boundary, Wheatley Road, Garsington, Oxford OX44
   9EJ, UK. UK and International radio and TV contact information.
*Writers and Artists Yearbook, The* (A & C Black, London). Annual reference source
   for British markets.

*Writers Handbook, The* (Macmillan, London). Annual reference source for British markets.

*Writer's Guide of South African Magazines, A* – Frances Roberts (Options Publishing).

*Writer's Market* (Writer's Digest, Cincinnati, Ohio). Annual reference source for American markets.

Writer's Digest Books are also distributed in UK, Canada, Australia and New Zealand. They also publish *Writer's Digest* and *Story* magazines, run the Writer's Digest School and have a criticism service. Full details available from: Writer's Digest, 1507 Dana Avenue, Cincinnati, Ohio 45207, USA. Call toll free (USA only) on: 1 800 289 0963. Web site: http:www.writersdigest.com

## Comedy writing

Allen, Steve, *How to be Funny* (Prometheus Books, USA; 1998).

Asa Berger, Arthur, *The Art of Comedy Writing* (Transactions Publishers, New Brunswick; 1997).

Helitzer, Melvyn, *Comedy Writing Secrets* (Writer's Digest, Cincinnati, Ohio; 1992).

Josephsburg, Milt, *Comedy Writing for Television and Hollywood* (Harper & Row Publishers, New York;1987).

Perret, Gene, *Comedy Writing Step by Step* (Samuel French Trade, New York; 1990).

Perret, Gene, *Comedy Writing Workbook* (Sterling/Cassell, New York; 1994).

Saks, Sol, *Funny Business, The Craft of Comedy Writing* (Lone Eagle Publishing Company, Los Angeles; 1991).

Schwarz, Lew, *The Craft of Writing TV Comedy* (Allison and Busby, London. 1988).

Wilde, Larry, (ed.) *How the Great Comedy Writers Create Laughter* (Nelson Hall Publishers, Chicago; 1976).

Wolfe, Ronald, *Writing Comedy: How to write scripts for TV, radio, film and stage* (Robert Hale, London; 1996).

Wolff, Jurgen, *Successful Sitcom Writing* (St Martin's Press, New York).

## Comedy history/background

Cook, William, (ed.) *Ha Bloody Ha* (Fourth Estate, London; 1994).

Clark, Andrew, S*tand and Deliver: Inside Canadian Comedy* (Bantam Books of Canada Ltd; 1997).

Elliott, Matt, *Kiwi Jokers: The Rise and Fall of New Zealand Comedy* (HarperCollins, Auckland).

Lewisohn, Mark, *Radio Times TV Comedy* (BBC Books, London; 1998).

Taylor, Rod, *The Guinness Book of Sitcoms* (Guinness Publishing, London; 1994).

Took, Barry, *Laughter In The Air: An Informal History of British Radio Comedy* (Robson Books/BBC, London; 1976).

Walke, John, (ed.) *Halliwell's Guide to the Best Comedies* (Harper Collins, London).

Wilmut, Roger, *From Fringe to Flying Circus: Celebrating a Unique Generation of Comedy 1960–1980* (Methuen, London, 1989). An examination of classic and ground breaking TV comedy series.

## Analysis of comedy

Goldstein, Jeffrey, and McGhee, Paul E, *The Psychology of Humour* (Academic Press, London; 1972).

Palmer, David J, *Comedy: Developments in Criticism: A Casebook* (Macmillan Education, Basingstoke, UK; 1984).

Palmer, Jerry, *Taking Humour Seriously* (Routledge, London; 1993).

## Scripts

Cleese, John and Booth, Connie *The Complete Fawlty Towers* (Methuen, London; 1988).

Harris, Susan, *The Golden Girls* (Boxtree, London, 1991). Ten scripts from the series.

Saunders, Jennifer, *Absolutely Fabulous* (Pocket Books, a division of Simon & Schuster Inc. New York, 1993; BBC Books, London, 1993; Penguin, 1995). The original six episodes.

Self, David, (ed.) *Studio Scripts, Sitcom 1 & 2* (Hutchinson Education, London; Century Hutchinson in Australia, New Zealand and South Africa). Study scripts of TV sitcoms for schools.

The following publishers have a selection of script books and TV tie-in titles.

BBC Books, 80 Wood Lane, London W12 0TT. Tel: 0181 576 2623. Publish TV tie-ins, script books etc.

Currency Press, 330 Oxford Street, Paddington, NSW 2021, Australia. Publish plays, TV scripts and books on the performing arts.

Robson Books, Bolsover House, 5–6 Clipstone Street, London W1P 7EB. Tel: 0171 323 1223.

## Comedy sketch/joke compilations

Brandreth, Giles, *Joke Box* (Puffin Books, Harmondsworth, UK; 1986. Also published by Viking Penguin in USA, and Penguin Books in Australia, New Zealand and Canada). Jokes and how to tell them. Intended for children but interesting.

Chapman, Graham, *et al*, *Monty Python's Flying Circus* (Mandarin, an imprint of Reed Consumer Books, London; 1990).

Muir, Frank and Brett, Simon (eds) *Penguin Book of Comedy Sketches* (Penguin, London). Comedy sketches from music hall, radio and television.

Various authors, *Amassed Hysteria* (Penguin, London). A compilation of sketches from the 'Hysteria' AIDS benefits.

## General writing books

Friedman, Julian, *How to Make Money Scriptwriting* (Boxtree, London). A guerrilla guide for selling to producers, script editors and agents in the film and TV industry, written by an agent.

Saunders, Jean, *How to Write Realistic Dialogue* (Allison & Busby, London; 1994).

St Maur, Suzan, *Write Your Own Scripts And Speeches* (McGraw Hill, Maidenhead, UK). Scripts and speeches for corporate TV, audio visual and live presentation.

Straczynski, J Michael, *The Complete Book of Scriptwriting* (Titan Books, London; 1997). Originally published by Writer's Digest, Cincinnati, Ohio). A guide to writing and selling screen and other plays, radio scripts and animation.

Swain, Dwight and R Swain, Joye, *Scripting for the New AV Technologies* (Focal Press, Boston; 1991).

Wigand, Molly, *How to Write and Sell Greetings Cards, Bumper Stickers, T-Shirts and Other Fun Stuff* (Writer's Digest, Cincinnati, Ohio; 1994).

Wolff, Jurgen and Cox, Kerry, *Successful Scriptwriting* (Writer's Digest, Cincinnati, Ohio; 1991). How to write and pitch scripts for movies, sitcoms, soaps and serials.

## Radio and television writing

Hilliard, Robert L, *Writing for Television and Radio* (Wadsworth Publishing; 1990).

Horstman, Rosemary, *Writing for Radio* (A & C Black, London; 1997).

Hulke, Malcolm, *Writing for Television in the 70s* (A & C Black, London; 1980). An older book but still valuable. Good examples on writing a script.

Kelsey, Gerald, *Writing for Television* (A & C Black, London; 1995).

Lucey, Paul, *Story Sense, A Screenwriter's Guide for Film and Television* (McGraw, New York; 1995).

Miller, William, *Screenwriting For Narrative Film and Television* (Virgin Publishing, London).

Paice, Eric, *The Way to Write for Television* (Elm Tree Books, London; 1987).

Richards, Keith, *Writing Radio Drama* (Currency Press, Sydney; 1991).

Smethurst, William, *How to Write for Television, A Complete Guide to Writing and Marketing TV Scripts* (How To Books, Oxford, UK; 1998).

Willis, Edgar E, *Writing Scripts for Television, Radio and Film* (Harcourt Brace Jovanovich College Publishing, San Diego; 1992).

## Television/video techniques

Izod, John, *Reading the Screen* (York Handbooks, Longman Press, Harlow, UK; 1984). Good for basic understanding of TV techniques.

McCrory, Nigel, *Shoot – How to Make a Video Film to Professional Standards* (Simon & Schuster, Hemel Hempstead, UK; 1993).

## Stand-up comedy

Carter, Judy, *Stand-up Comedy – the Book* (Dell Trade Paperback, New York; 1989). The nuts and bolts of writing and performing stand-up comedy.

Double, Oliver, *Stand-up: On Being a Comedian* (Methuen, an imprint of Reed Consumer Books, London, 1998). An analysis of the background to stand-up and a serious exploration of the life of a comedian.

Perret, Gene, *Successful Stand-up Comedy: Advice from a Comedy Writer* (Samuel French Trade, New York; 1994).

## Contacting comedians

*Artistes and their Agents*, Richmond House Publishing, Douglas House, 3 Richmond Buildings, London W1V 5AE, UK. Tel: 0171 437 9556 Fax: 0171 287 3463.

*Contacts*, published annually by Spotlight, 7 Leicester Place, London WC2H 7BP, UK. Tel: 0171 437 7631.

*Showcall*, two volume edition published by The Stage, 47 Bermondsey Street, London SE1 3XT, UK.

## Cartooning, animation

Brooks, Clive, *The Way to Write Comics* (Elm Tree Books, London).

Haines, Lurene, *The Writer's Guide to the Business of Comics* (Watson-Guptill Publications, New York; 1998).

Taylor, Dave, *A Guide to Comic Scripting* (Hale, London; 1993).

Taylor, Richard, *The Encyclopaedia of Animation Techniques* (Focal Press imprint of Reed International Books, London; 1996).

Whitaker, Steve, *The Encyclopaedia of Cartoon Techniques* (Headline, London; 1996).

## Writing for children

De Gale, Ann, *Writing for the Teenage Market* (A & C Black, London; 1993).

Krailing, Tessa, *How to Write for Children* (Allison & Busby, London; 1996).

Seuling, Barbara, *How to Write a Children's Book & Get it Published* (Charles Schribner's Sons, New York; 1991).

Taylor, Jennifer, *Writing Children's Books That Sell* (Writer's Digest, Cincinnati, Ohio, 1996; Hale, London, 1999).

Wyndham, Lee, *Writing for Children and Teenagers* (Writer's Digest, Cincinnati, Ohio; 1991).

# Magazines

## Comedy publications

*The Oldie*, 45–6 Poland Street, London W1V 4AU, UK Tel: 0171 734 2225. Monthly humour magazine for the older person.

*MAD magazine*, 485 Madison Avenue, New York, NY 10022, USA. Web site: http://www.dccomics.com/mad/index.html Published eight times a year.

*National Lampoon*, National Lampoon Inc., 155 Avenue of the Americas, New York, NY 10013, USA. Tel: 212 645 5040.

*Private Eye*, 6 Carlisle Street, London W1V 5RG, UK. Tel: 0171 437 4017. Fortnightly satirical and investigative magazine.

*Punch*, Trevor House, 100 Brompton Road, London SW3 1ER, UK. Tel: 0171 225 6848. Weekly upmarket humour magazine.

## General

*Children's Book Insider*, 254 E Mombasha Road, Monroe, NY 10950, USA.

*Progressive Greetings Magazine*, Max Publishing Ltd., United House, North Road, London N7 9DP, UK. Tel: 0171 700 6740.

*Writer's News*, PO Box 4, Nairn, Scotland IV12 4HU. Tel: 01667 454441. Fax: 01667 454401. Monthly subscription only, markets, news, features, contests.

*Writer's World*, PO Box 1588, Somerset West, 7129, South Africa. Tel: 024 852 4728. Fax: 024-51-2592.

*Writing*, address as *Writer's News*. Bi-monthly, features, interviews and contests.

# Useful information

## Recordings suppliers

The BBC Radio Collection, PO Box 190, Peterborough PE2 6UW, UK. Tel: 0181 576 2210. Radio comedy and comedians.

Laughing Stock, Tiptree Book Services, Church Road, Tiptree, Essex CO5 0SR, UK. Tel: 01621 819600. Fax: 01621 819717. Overseas orders to: Random House UK Ltd, International Sales Dept., 20 Vauxhall Bridge Road, London SW1V 2SA, UK. Tel: 0171 973 9000. Fax: 0171 233 7031. Audio cassette recordings of TV series and comedians.

Talking Tapes Direct, Freepost (PE 564) Peterborough PE2 6BR. e-mail: orders@talkingtapesdirect.co.uk Web site: www.talkingtapesdirect.co.uk Amongst the list are classic UK comedy compilations, comedians, TV shows.

## Specialist bookshops

Larry Edmonds Bookshop, 6658 Hollywood Boulevard, Hollywood, CA 90028, USA.

The Lighter Side, 47 Upper Richmond West, East Sheen, London SW14, UK. Tel: 0181 876 6045. Specializes in humour books.

Offstage Theatre and Cinema Bookshop, 37 Chalk Farm Road, London NW1 8AJ, UK. Tel: 0171 485 4996.

Screenwriter's Store, PO Box 11008, London SE10 9ZH, UK. Tel/Fax: 0181 293 1144.

The Writer's Computer Store, 11317 Santa Monica Boulevard, Los Angeles, CA 90025–3118, USA. Tel: 310 479 7774. Fax: 310 477 5314
Web site: http://writerscomputerstore.com/store/comedy_writing_books.htm

Kip's Comedy Bookstore, USA based on-line resource: http://kipaddotta.com/

## Course and seminar organizers

The Arvon Foundation, Totleigh Barton, Sheepwash, Beaworthy, Devon EX21 5NS, UK. Tel: 01409 23338. Long established, courses in all writing genres. Centres also at Hebden Bridge, Yorkshire and Beauly, Invernesshire.

Greg Dean Workshops, PO Box 2929, Hollywood, CA 90078–2929, USA. Tel: 310 285 3799.

Kent Enterprises, The Oast House, Plaxtol, Sevenoaks, Kent, UK. TN15 0QG, UK. Tel: 01732 810632. Residential workshops in comedy writing, screenwriting, story structure.

Laugh Lines, 1/24 Akatea Street, Berhampore, Wellington, New Zealand. Tel: 04 380 1133. Fax: 04 380 1144. e-mail: laflines@ihug.co.az Stand-up comedy courses/workshops to order.

The Leisure Study Group International, Tuition House, 44 Main Street, Howick 3290, South Africa. Tel: 332 304 880. Fax: 332 305 195. Web site: http://www.lsgi.co.za Correspondence courses.

## Internet web sites

http://britishtheatre.miningco.com/mlibrary.htm (British theatre companies, theatres, actors, writers).

http://entertainment.iafrica.com/tv/comedy.htm (South African TV comedy programmes).

http://members.xoom.com/ralanconley (Ralan Conley's Humor Market).

http://members.aol.com/comicbible/index.html (Information for comedians, writers).

http://tvtp.simplenet.com/ (The Television Transcript Project. Lots of sitcom and other TV transcripts).

http://writers.ngapartji.com.au/linx.Austlinx.htm (Australian writers' links).

http://www.bizsa.com/bizsa/biz/freel.htm (South African media resource).

http://www.comedycafe.com.au/funny_links.html (Australian, USA and world comedy links).

http://www.darkin.demon.co.uk (Excellent site for guidelines, markets and information on UK radio, TV, theatre).

http://www.earthchannel.com/comedymg/ (The Comedy Magazine).

http://www.geocities.com/TelevisionCity/Set/5799/ (Scripts for sitcom 'Friends').

http://www.kelly.mcmail.com (Comedy and drama writing).

http://www.man.ac.uk/~zlsiida.sitcom.index.html (Definitive UK Sitcom List).

http://www.mediauk.com/directory (Media UK Internet Directory).

http://www.prairienet.org/britcom/BD/ (Britcomedy Digest, on-line magazine).

http://www.prairienet.org/rec/britcom/specific.htm/ (Prairienet British Comedy Clearing House. Links to lots of shows and performers).

http://www.radio411.com/africa.htm (South African radio stations).

http://www.script-o-rama (Drew's scriptorama. Over 600 scripts).

http://www.surtfpoint.com/movies_Comedy (Links to comedy information).

http://www.write4kids.com (Children's Writing Resource Centre).

# INDEX